THE RISE OF COMMUNIST CHINA

MODERN WORLD PROBLEMS

greenhaven press, inc.

577 Shoreview Park Road, St. Paul, Minnesota 55112

The Modern World Problems series was developed by the British Schools Council which was established by the British Department of Education and Science in cooperation with teacher organizations to develop innovative materials for the teaching of history. Greenhaven Press is pleased to offer this outstanding book series to American teachers and librarians for the study of world issues and social conflicts. The series is published in Great Britain by Holmes McDougall Ltd.

Project Team

David Sylvester *(Director to 1975)*
Tony Boddington *(Director 1975-1977)*
Gwenifer Griffiths *(1975-1976)*
William Harrison *(1972-1975)*
John Mann *(1974-1975)*
Aileen Plummer *(1972-1977)*
Denis Shemilt *(Evaluator 1974-1977)*
Peter Wenham *(to 1974)*

Design by George Nicol/Forth Studios
Picture research by Procaudio Limited

ISBN 0-912616-69-5 Paper Edition
ISBN 0-912616-70-9 Library Edition

CONTENTS

INTRODUCTION

Let China sleep. When she wakes, the
world will be sorry.   (*Napoleon*)

China is a vast country. The land is larger than the whole continent of Europe and the Mediterranean Sea combined. Out of all the people in the world, one person in four is Chinese.

Chinese civilisation is ancient. The Chinese were studying medicine, mathematics, engineering and astronomy at a time when primitive hunters roamed in Britain.

Yet this vast and ancient country exercised little influence on the world outside her own borders until recent times. China was like a sleeping giant.

This is not true today. Communist China is now a power in the world. She was admitted to the United Nations in 1971 and is a permanent member of the Security Council. Her industry is developing rapidly. She possesses her own nuclear weapons. Like America and the Soviet Union she gives aid to the poorer countries of Asia, Africa and South America.

How has this change been brought about?

The awakening became obvious to most people in the west when the Communists came to power in China in 1949. But, for more than 100 years before that, changes had been occurring in China, and for half a century revolutionaries had tried to change the country completely. In order to understand how China became Communist we must look first at some of the earlier movements for reform and see just what kinds of changes people wanted.

Bronze leopards, about 2000 years old

White pottery jug, 4000–5000 years old

The Great Wall of China

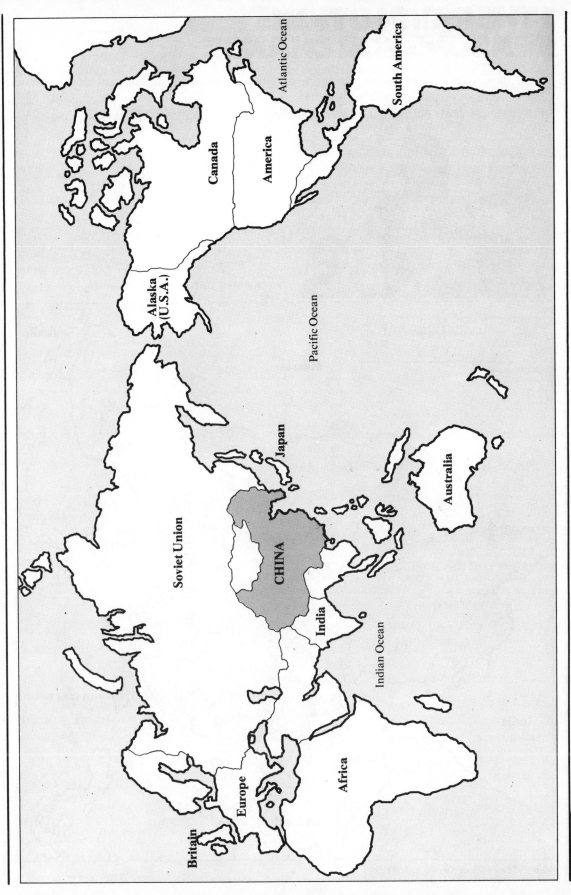

Map 1: China's position in the world today

1 THE REVOLUTION: REASONS FOR CHANGE

During the nineteenth century Europeans came to China as traders and as Christian missionaries, so Chinese officials learned something about western technology and forms of government. After rebellions in the 1850s and 1860s the government began what was called a "self-strengthening move-

Typical peasant family in pre-Communist China

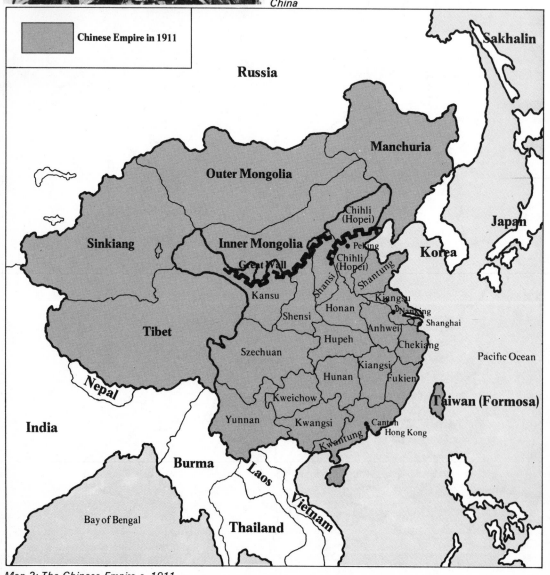

Map 2: The Chinese Empire c. 1911

ment" to restore order. The idea was to make China strong by copying and using western ideas and western arms and machines (Sources 1 and 2). However, China did not become strong. Most of her people were very poor and had to struggle to live, so it is not surprising that many felt resentful of the riches and power which the foreigners seemed to enjoy.

English officer drilling Chinese soldiers at Amoy, 1875

Source 1

I know that within a hundred years China will adopt all Western methods and excel in them . . . If China does not make a change at this time, how can she be on a par with the great nations of Europe, and compare with them in power and strength?

(Wang Tao, 1828–1897)

Source 2

We have only one thing to learn from the Barbarians [foreigners], and that is strong ships and effective guns . . . Funds should be allocated to establish a shipyard and arsenal in each trading port. A few Barbarians should be employed, and Chinese who are good in using their minds should be selected to receive instruction so that in turn they may teach many craftsmen.

(Feng Kuei-fen, 1809–1847)

Map 3: The geography of China

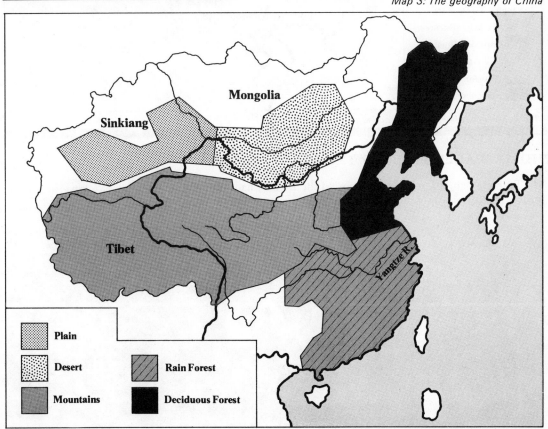

Plain

Desert

Mountains

Rain Forest

Deciduous Forest

THE BOXER REBELLION

Secret societies had always been common in China and in 1895 one was formed which we usually call "the Boxers". Its Chinese name means "the Society of the Righteous Harmony Fists" and its aim was 'to protect the country, destroy the foreigner'. For two months in the summer of 1900 the Boxers besieged the foreign legations in Peking and altogether about 240 foreigners were killed in North China and Manchuria. The government quickly declared that this had been just a secret society revolt, not an anti-foreigner war, but the Chinese were made to apologise to the countries whose citizens had been killed and to pay compensation. In addition they were not to import any arms or munitions for two years. China felt disgraced and humiliated, and the Empress, who had at first supported the Boxers, felt driven to introduce some changes which she had resisted for years.

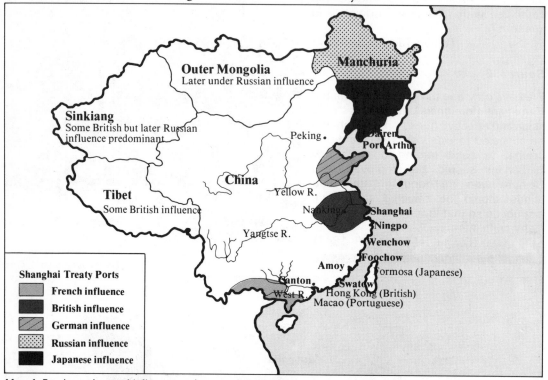

Map 4: Foreign spheres of influence and treaty ports c. 1911

THE DOWAGER EMPRESS TZU HSI

The Empress Tzu Hsi, who had supported the Boxers, had been the virtual ruler of China since 1861, in 1898 she had actually imprisoned the Emperor. She was the last effective ruler of the Manchu dynasty

A Mandarin of 70 years ago

and has been accused of dreadful cruelty and of putting her personal ambitions before the good of China (Source 3). However, she was a woman of great charm and there is no doubt that she was admired by many of her subjects, especially in the area around Peking (Source 4).

BIOGRAPHY: THE EMPRESS TZU-HSI

Tzu-hsi was born in 1835, the daughter of a Mandarin (an official in the imperial civil service). Her family were members of the ruling class of China, the Manchus. The Manchus came originally from Manchuria and had invaded China in the seventeenth century. Manchu emperors ruled China for the next 250 years. Although in time they were greatly influenced by the Chinese way of life, the Manchus tried to retain and emphasise the differences between themselves, as a ruling race, and their Chinese subjects. The emperors encouraged Manchu families to retain their own language and customs. Inter-marriage with Chinese was discouraged. Even the emperors were forbidden to marry Chinese subjects and so only Manchu girls were eligible for service in the Forbidden City in Peking as concubines of the Emperor.

In 1851 at the age of 16, Tzu-hsi was summoned to join the harem of the young Hsien-feng Emperor in Peking. In 1856 she gave birth to a son, the Emperor's only male heir. When the Emperor died in 1861, Tzu-hsi ensured by clever intrigue that her five year old son was named as his successor. After months of clever plotting Tzu-hsi also managed to gain effective control of the regency government. Women were, in fact, forbidden to rule in China and so Tzu-hsi conducted state business from behind imperial yellow curtains. Her regency government became known as "Listening Behind Screens to Reports on Government Affairs". Even when her son, the Tung-Chih Emperor, was old enough to govern alone Tzu-hsi continued to direct state affairs.

In 1875 when her son died, Tzu-hsi adopted her three year old nephew and, violating the succession laws, she named him the new Emperor, Kuang-hsu. Tzu-hsi retained control of the government.

During the years of Tzu-hsi's rule, some steps were taken to modernise China by developing industry and building railways. But little was done to prevent corruption amongst government officials or to improve the lives of the mass of Chinese peasants. While her subjects paid heavy taxes, Tzu-hsi lived a life of extravagance and luxury in the Forbidden City, isolated from the world outside. She even used money intended for the navy to rebuild the magnificent summer palace outside Peking.

In 1898 after the Chinese forces were badly defeated in a war with the Japanese, the young Kuang-hsu Emperor tried to introduce government reforms. Tzu-hsi, however, with the support of conservative government officials reversed the reforms and imprisoned the Emperor in his palace. She then resumed control of the government. Most historians believed that this was the end of China's last chance for peaceful change. Tzu-hsi's attempts at reform after the Boxer rebellion in 1900 came too late. As one historian has commented, Tzu-hsi was "one of the most powerful women in Chinese history" but she "contributed nothing to the welfare either of China or the Manchu dynasty".

The Empress ruled through an organisation of civil servants, called mandarins. Nearly all the mandarins came from rich landowning families, because if a boy was to pass the complicated and difficult examinations to become a mandarin he must have an expensive education. Shielded from ordinary people by her rich court in the Forbidden City in Peking, Tzu-hsi was completely out of touch with the life of hard physical labour and the constant threat of starvation which most of her subjects faced. Many people realised this and demands for change were aimed not just against foreigners but against the Manchu dynasty itself.

After the failure of the Boxer rebellion, Tzu-hsi, to save her own skin, introduced reforms. The entrance examination for the civil service was abolished and more schools were to be built. In 1908 the government promised that within a year an assembly should be elected in each province and the following year there would be elections for a national assembly which would advise the government. Eventually there was to be a parliament which would make laws. But in November 1908 the Dowager Empress Tzu-hsi died, a few hours after the still-imprisoned Emperor. The new Emperor, the three-year-old Pu-yi, had little chance of holding together the crumbling dynasty. On 10 October 1911 (known as the Double Tenth) it was shattered by revolution and the republic began.

Source 3

THE DOWAGER EMPRESS TZU-HSI

When she sent a man to death, it was because he stood between her and the full and safe gratification of her love of power. When her fierce rage was turned against the insolence of the foreigner, she had no scruple in consigning every European in China to the executioner; . . . but in every recorded instance, except one, her methods were swift, clean, and, from the Oriental point of view, not unmerciful. She had no liking for tortures, or the lingering death.

(from J. O. P. Bland and E. Backhouse, *China under the Empress Dowager,* Heinemann,1910, pp. 480 –481)

Source 4

[Tzu-hsi] was at once a child and a woman . . . She would go into the Audience Hall, transact weighty affairs of State for three hours, and then go for her walks or excursions, and take a childish interest in the simplest pleasures. She would be seated in one of her throne rooms in trivial conversation with her ladies, when an Official Despatch, in its yellow silk case, would be brought in. Her face would immediately become full of serious interest; a few moments later she became again the woman, full of interest in her flowers, dresses and jewels.

(from Katherine A. Carl, *With the Empress Dowager of China,* Eveleigh Nash,1906, p. 101)

The Emperor Pu-yi

SUN YAT-SEN AND THE NEW CHINESE REPUBLIC

Many groups had plotted and tried to overthrow the Dowager Empress and the dynasty, but at Tzu Hsi's death no-one seemed more likely to succeed than Sun Yat-sen. He was a distinguished doctor, but the misery and corruption he saw in Canton made him decide to give up medicine and devote himself to politics. At first he believed the government could be persuaded to make changes, but when reports which he and his friends wrote were ignored, he realised that revolution would be necessary. In 1895 his first attempt at rebellion failed and he left the country, eventually settling for a while in England.

Although his planned rebellion had failed, the Chinese government must have regarded him as a threat. While he was staying in London in lodgings found by his friend and former tutor, Dr James Cantlie, officials at the Chinese Legation kidnapped him. Luckily for him, he managed to get a note out to Dr Cantlie. Sun Yat-sen was saved from deportation to China and death by the intervention of the Prime Minister, Lord Salisbury, and the London crowds who gathered outside the Chinese Legation. The Chinese government felt it could not afford to let relations with Britain deteriorate further, and Sun was released.

During the next two years Sun lived in London and spent much of his time at the British Museum, where he studied the writings of Karl Marx. The Communist leaders of the Russian Revolution were strongly influenced by Marx and it was after this period of study that Sun began to work out just what changes were needed in China. At first he had wanted to overthrow the dynasty without being sure what would replace it. While he was in Japan in 1905 he formed a new political party, the Tung Meng Hui (the Chinese Revolutionary Alliance). This aimed at friendship with other countries, the creation of a Chinese republic, and the nationalisation of land, in contrast to the existing system of landlords and peasants.

Several unsuccessful attempts at rebellion were made, but Sun was on one of his many fund-raising tours abroad when the revolution of the Double Tenth began in 1911. He did not get back to China till December, but he had already been chosen as Provisional President of the new Republic of China, which was proclaimed on 1 January 1912. However, for the sake of peace in China, when the child-Emperor abdicated, Yuan Shih-kai, commander of the army, was declared President. Sun thought that Yuan shared many of his ideas. In fact, Yuan did not believe in the revolution and his attempts to restore strong government brought disunity and strife to China. Nothing was solved by his death in 1916. His

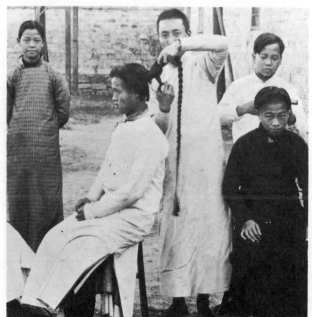

Sun Yat-sen, 1914

Cutting pig-tails in the streets during the 1911 revolution: pig-tails were a symbol of foreign oppression to the Chinese, because they had been ordered to wear them by the Manchu emperors. The emperors had come from Manchuria and conquered China 300 years earlier

BIOGRAPHY: YUAN SHI-KAI (1859-1916)

Yuan Shi-kai was a farmer's son, born in the Hunan province in 1859. As a young boy Yuan was adopted by a local general and he later joined the army. He fought in Korea against the Japanese in 1882 and proved himself an outstanding soldier. In 1895 at the age of 36 he was asked to organise and command a new imperial army. The Dowager Empress Tzu-hsi wanted to use this army to maintain her own power against her enemies and so she cultivated the friendship of Yuan Shi-kai. His troops successfully suppressed the Boxer rebels in 1900 and in 1901 Yuan was made Viceroy of the province around Peking.

On the death of Tzu-hsi in 1908, Yuan lost his power and was removed from office. In 1911, however, when the revolution broke out he challenged Sun Yat-sen for the leadership of China. Sun Yat-sen wanted to create a democratic government but Yuan Shi-kai was convinced that dictatorship was the key to China's national recovery. He had the support of the strongest army divisions and of most of the northern provinces.

In the face of civil war Sun Yat-sen decided not to oppose Yuan Shi-kai. Yuan then became the first President of the Republic of China. He quickly undermined the authority of the new national assembly, ignoring the wishes of the majority Kuomintang party. After the murder of the Kuomintang leader, civil war broke out. Yuan's control over the northern army enabled him to crush opposition throughout most of China.

In 1913 Yuan Shi-kai forced the national assembly to appoint him President for life and in 1915 established himself as the new Emperor of China. This provoked a new rebellion. To save himself he agreed to abdicate and withdrew from public life. He died in June 1916, a broken man.

official successor, Li Yuan-hung, ruled in Peking and Sun established a government of sorts in Canton. Most of the country, however, was ruled by local leaders, known as 'Warlords'. These were soldiers who organised their own small armies and terrorised local areas, usually for their own profit.

To make matters worse, Japan took advantage of China's weakness. In 1915, Japan presented the 'Twenty-one Demands'. These gave her a great measure of control over the life and work of the Chinese people, especially in the north (Source 5).

Li Yuan-hung

Chang Tso-lin, the shepherd boy who rose to be a Warlord

EXTRACTS FROM THE TWENTY-ONE DEMANDS

II

ARTICLE V. The Chinese government agrees that in respect of the two cases mentioned herein below, the Japanese government consent shall be first obtained before action is taken:

(a) Whenever permission is granted to the subject of a third Power to build a railway or to make a loan with a third Power for the purpose of building a railway in South Manchuria and Eastern Inner Mongolia.

(b) Whenever a loan is to be made with a third Power pledging the local taxes of South Manchuria and Eastern Inner Mongolia as security.

ARTICLE VI. The Chinese government agrees that if the Chinese government employs political, financial or military advisers, or instructors in South Manchuria or Eastern Inner Mongolia, the Japanese government shall first be consulted.

V.

ARTICLE I. The Chinese central government shall employ influential Japanese as advisers in political, financial, and military affairs.

ARTICLE IV. China shall purchase from Japan a fixed amount of munitions of war (say 50 per cent or more of what is needed by the Chinese government) or that there shall be established in China a Sino-Japanese jointly worked arsenal. Japanese technic-experts are to be employed and Japanese material to be purchased.

(quoted in Charles Meyer and Ian Allen, *Source Materials in Chinese History*, Frederick Warne, 1970, pp. 120–1)

THE MAY FOURTH MOVEMENT

The misery and humiliation that the Chinese were forced to suffer led to a series of demonstrations throughout the country, beginning in Peking on 4 May 1919. Some students were wounded and a few

The 'May 4' demonstration

were killed and the prisons were soon full of demonstrators. The immediate cause of their demonstration had been the decision at the peace conference following the First World War to leave part of Shantung in Japanese hands. But anti-Japanese feeling was only one reason for what became known as 'The May Fourth Movement'. Scholars and students realised that attempts to copy western ideas or to form a strong government had so far failed in China. It was time the Chinese looked carefully at their own traditions and institutions and made changes which would suit China (Source 6). The scholars gained the support of merchants and industrial workers and, although revolution did not follow immediately, this was the beginning of a nationalist movement which would grow in the 1920s.

Source 6

PART OF AN ARTICLE WRITTEN BY THE YOUNG MAO TSE-TUNG IN 1919

All you gentlemen who cultivate the land ! How do the landlords treat us ? Are the rents and taxes heavy or light ? Are our houses satisfactory or not ? Are our bellies full or not ? Is there enough land ? Are there not some in the village who have no land to cultivate ? We must constantly seek solutions to these problems. We must establish a union with others like ourselves, to seek clear and effective solutions.

Gentlemen ! We are workers. We wish to form a union with others who work like ourselves, in order to promote the various interests of us workers. We cannot fail to seek a solution to such problems concerning us workers as the level of our wages, the length of the working day, the equal or unequal sharing of dividends, or the progress of amusement facilities. We cannot but establish a union with those like ourselves to seek clear and effective solutions to each of these problems.

(*The Great Union of the Popular Masses,* July 1919)

Mao in 1919

THE CHINESE COMMUNIST PARTY

Although attempts to copy western styles of government had not worked in China, there was one country which seemed likely to offer an example to China. In 1917 revolution had broken out in Russia and, after fighting a civil war, the Bolsheviks had succeeded in establishing a Communist state. It seemed to Sun Yat-sen that they believed in many things which he and his party wanted in China. The state had taken over the ownership of all land and redistributed it amongst the peasants. Industry too was state-owned so that profits could be used to improve production and be shared equally amongst the workers, rather than go into the pockets of a small number of men. Sun appealed to Lenin, the Bolshevik leader, for help. In 1922 and 1923 a number of Russian advisers came to China to help Sun to reorganise his party, the Kuomintang (the old Tung Meng Hui), on more strictly disciplined lines.

In 1921 the Chinese Communist Party (CCP) had been formed and soon the young Mao Tse-tung became one of its leading members. From the original six small groups the party grew and other groups were organised in cities and villages. Governing them all was the Central Party Committee, which worked to spread Communism throughout China. Marx had believed that a society based on a small number of rich landowners and a large number of peasants would be replaced by an industrial society where power was in the hands of people with money to invest in industry (capitalists). This kind of society must in turn be replaced by a more just society. Power would be in the hands of people who worked in the mines, mills and factories to produce the goods which made the country more prosperous. Such a change could be brought about only by revolution, because no capitalists could be expected to give up their wealth and power willingly to the workers. Such a revolution was what the CCP wanted in China.

Young Mao with a group of fellow Communists (second from left)

THE KUOMINTANG

Sun's party, the Kuomintang (KMT), welcomed the help of the CCP because they felt it would help them to develop an efficient organisation and so gain control over the whole country. They also believed that, up to a point, their aims were similar. Sun had formulated what he called the *Three Principles of the People*. One of these, *the People's Livelihood*, was rather vague but it certainly included the intention that private ownership of land and factories should be abolished and that there should not be big differences in income. The other two Principles were *Nationalism* and *Democracy*. At first Nationalism had meant the end of Manchu rule. That had already been achieved and Sun now aimed

Foreign influence: Chinese children in European dress

at ending foreign influence so that the people of China should be ruled by a Chinese government which was not in any way responsible to Japan or any European country. By Democracy he meant that all citizens should, through free elections, have some part in the government of the country. But he now admitted that this was something to work for in the future. In the early 1920s the priority must be to rule the country effectively and it seemed that free elections must wait until the KMT governed the whole of China.

COOPERATION BETWEEN THE KMT AND THE CCP

Sun did not believe that Communism was the answer for China and he realised that in any case most Chinese were peasants working on the land. So China's society was not at the industrial capitalist stage which Marx had described as the preliminary to revolution. But, as we have seen, the KMT was glad of the help of the Communists, although at first the Communists themselves wanted to remain separate because they recognised that the aims of the CCP were in fact far more revolutionary than those of the KMT. However, partly on the advice of the Russians, the Chinese Communists agreed to join the KMT. They saw that they were not strong enough on their own to bring about revolution in China, but as members of the KMT they could work to take over the government from within. Whether Sun could have made these two groups work effectively together we do not know. There had been time to establish only the organisation when Sun died in March 1925.

Bearers carrying the body of Sun Yat-sen to the purple mountain outside Nanking where the burial took place in a magnificent tomb next to those of the Ming Emperors

CHIANG KAI-SHEK

After Sun Yat-sen's death General Chiang Kai-shek became the new leader of the KMT. Most of China was still controlled by the Warlords and Chiang immediately set about the task of subduing them. At first, he was successful but, by 1927, deep divisions appeared within the Kuomintang. The Communists were using Chiang's victories to encourage the peasants to rise against their landlords and the town workers against their employers. Chiang decided that he needed the support of the foreign merchants and bankers who were being threatened by the Communists. He expelled his Russian advisers and began a campaign of terror to destroy the Communist revolutionary leaders (Sources 7, 8).

Mao Tse-tung realised that he was not strong enough to withstand the Kuomintang forces. He withdrew to a remote area of Kiangsi to reorganise the Red Army, which was to be the spearhead of the Communist revolution.

BIOGRAPHY: CHIANG KAI-SHEK (1887-1975) THE EARLY YEARS

Chiang Kai-shek was born in 1887 in the coastal province of Chekiang. His family were prosperous merchants and farmers. As a young man he attended military academies in China and in Japan. From 1909–11 he served in the Japanese army and was greatly influenced by its Spartan discipline and ideals. While in Japan he became convinced that the powers of the Manchu emperors should be abolished and that China should become a republic.

In 1911 when the revolution began in China, Chiang returned home and was involved in the fighting which led to the overthrow of the Manchu dynasty. In 1912–13 he also took part in plots against Yuan Shi-kai, the first president of the Chinese Republic, who tried to make himself the new Emperor.

In 1918 after Yuan Shi-kai's death, Chiang joined Sun Yat-sen the leader of the Nationalist Party (Kuomintang). Sun Yat-sen was trying to re-unite China and end the fighting between the Warlords in the provinces. Chiang went to southern China as a major general to try to gain control of the Warlords' armies but he had no success.

Chiang soon realised that if the Nationalist Party was to gain control of China, it must have its own army. To do this the Nationalists needed foreign help. In 1923, therefore, Chiang visited the Soviet Union to study the Russian 'Red Army'. On his return to China, Chiang established a Russian-type military academy at Whampoa near Canton. Here he began to build up a KMT army. Russian advisers flooded into Canton and Chinese Communists were allowed to join the KMT. Chiang himself was influenced by the ideas of Karl Marx and Lenin but he never became a Communist. On Sun Yat-sen's death, Chiang, with the support of the Whampoa army behind him, became the new Nationalist leader.

Communists executed by the KMT in Canton, 1928

Soon, the Red Army was ready to occupy the whole province of Kiangsi. The peasants, assured of protection against the Kuomintang, drove away the landlords and took their land to share between them (Source 9). Chiang Kai-shek attacked the Red Army in four different campaigns from 1931 onwards.

When these all ended in failure, he surrounded the Communists, determined to starve them into surrender. The only way that the Red Army could survive was to break out of this blockade and set up a new base in a place of safety a long way away. Carrying the minimum of belongings, Mao and his fellow-revolutionaries broke through where Chiang's forces were weakest. This was the beginning of one of the most dramatic and hazardous adventures in history; the Long March had begun.

Source 7

AN ACCOUNT OF THE MASSACRE OF THE COMMUNISTS IN CANTON IN 1927

The Communist plan was to coordinate an insurrection in Canton with a general peasant uprising through Kwangtung. It was calculated that the peasant revolt would force Li Chi-shen to withdraw part of his forces from the city and thus facilitate its seizure by the Communists...

Just at that time the Chinese Chief of Police in Canton discovered the conspiracy, however, and ordered the arrest of all Communist labour union members. It was evident that a conflict was about to break, and tension began to rise throughout the city. Frederick W. Hinke, an American Vice-Consul, described it in a report . . . shooting broke out in the city just before dawn, but it was not yet clear what had taken place. As foreigners on Shameen came out to take their customary Sunday morning stroll they were bewildered by the numbers of cargo boats and sampans massed against the island where the concessions were located. 'When the sampans move out of the canal which separates Shameen from the city of Canton proper,' Hinke observed, 'it is a sure sign of trouble.'

. . . by noon the Communists controlled Canton. A soviet of workers', soldiers', and peasants' deputies was chosen with ten delegates from labour groups and three from each of the other two categories.

Canton under Communist domination November 1925: a procession of strikers passes through the streets

Confusion had seized the city, rebel squads and aimless crowds surged in the streets. The killing was brutal and indiscriminate, but anti-Communist forces were soon to achieve 'an eye-for-an-eye and a tooth-for-a-tooth' revenge.

For purposes of identification the Communists had adopted a red sash and red ties. And since the weather was warm, and as the wearers perspired, the dye discoloured their necks. Near the heart of Canton a wildly excited, bobbed haired Chinese girl waved a rifle above her head and harangued the mob.

Communist forces held Canton for two days. Then Chang Fak-uei's 'Ironsides' units opened attack. 'The so-called White troops entered the city so quickly that the Russian Vice-Consul and an assistant were caught in front of the Communist headquarters with a red flag on the consulate car. The inmates of the consulate were immediately arrested, and five members, two of whom were peasant organisers of the consulate staff, were shot.'

When the Communists saw that they were losing the fight, they began discarding sashes and ties, but the tell-tale dye stains would not wipe off.

'Execution squads patrolled the streets', reported Vice-Consul Hinke, 'and on finding a suspect, they questioned him, examined his neck for the tell-tale red. If found, they ordered the victim to open his mouth, thrust a revolver into it, and another coolie came to the end of his Communist venture.'

There seemed to be no end to the killing. 'I, myself, saw a rickshaw stopped, the coolie grabbed by the police, his shirt jerked from his neck disclosing the red stain . . .' Hinke recalled. 'He was rushed to the side of the road, compelled to kneel down, and unceremoniously shot while the crowd of people in the street applauded.

Everywhere was the odour of fire and corpses . . . One picked one's way carefully . . . Police directed gangs of coolies who were collecting the bodies of the executed into trucks. Some of the victims . . . were still quivering.'

Fires broke out in the city. 'The richest shops in Canton were looted, some as many as eighteen times in a single night, until every scrap of goods was removed, together even with the scales, yard sticks, brass cuspidors, and the show cases were smashed.'

The city was terrorised by the senseless killing and by the fires which raged through the night.

'Many private scores were paid off', according to another American consular officer, Jay Calvin Huston. 'Two lots of 500 and 1000 men each were taken out and machine gunned. Realising that this was a waste of ammunition, the soldiers loaded the victims on boats, took them down the river below the city, and pushed them overboard in lots of ten or twelve men tied together. The slaughter continued for four or five days during which some 6000 people, allegedly Communists, lost their lives in the city of Canton.'

(from R. C. North, *Chinese Communism*, Weidenfeld and Nicolson, 1969, pp. 101–4)

TERROR TACTICS AGAINST THE COMMUNISTS IN PEKING

Peking. April 29.

The execution of 20 Communists by strangulation yesterday was carried out in circumstances of great brutality. It appears to have been a deliberately slow process, each case taking about ten minutes.

(*The Times,* Saturday 30 April, 1927)

Source 9

THE RED ARMY WINS THE SUPPORT OF THE PEASANTS

In 1935 an army calling itself the Red Army arrived. It was in the countryside. The KMT was in the towns . . .

. . . in April 1935 the Red Army defeated an armed counter-revolutionary land-owners' corps ten li [about 5 km] from here . . . Then the people saw that the Red Army did have power, and so we stopped driving into the town with our taxes and goods. Instead, we organised ourselves into guer-rilla bands. Eight to ten men to each . . .

The first big action I took part in was in May 1935. We had a message that we were to do in a landowner who would not surrender voluntarily. We came walking along all the paths with red flags on our spears. The landowner's name was Ma Sho-yen and he was all-powerful in Tseu-sanyan village.

He had now barricaded himself in his house and had twenty armed men round him to defend his property. These were his own tenants, and it was their duty to defend him.

We had only twenty Red Army men, but the Self-defence Corps from all the villages had come too. The landowner's house was now surrounded by hundreds of men. We set up red flags on all the hills round about and there were lots of them, so the horizon was quite red all round Ma Sho-yen. Then we all called to the land-owner and held up our spears and said: 'If you don't give us your land and if you don't give us your rifles, you won't survive. You will die tonight.' After a while he came out. He was a big man in his fifties with a moustache, and he said: 'As long as I can keep my life, the land and rifles don't matter.' When we had got the rifles, we let him go off and he ran away to Kanchuan. No-one was even wounded in that action. And as soon as the landowner had fled, the villagers emerged; you see, they had been forced to stay with the landowner because they were afraid he would report them as 'bandits' or 'Red Army-men' and he had told them that if he did that, the KMT would cut off their heads.

They were glad now and we held a big meeting and divided the land up and all the landowner's possessions.

(Jan Myrdal, *Report from a Chinese Village,* Heinemann, 1965, pp. 68–9)

A peasant defence corps

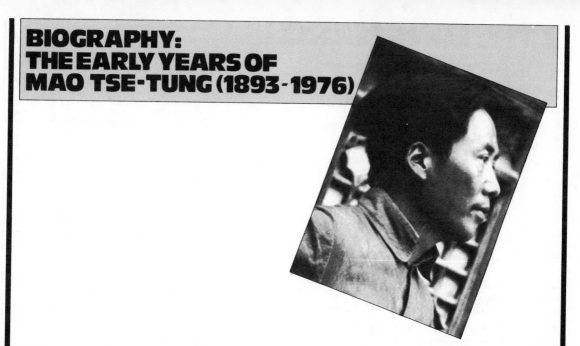

Mao Tse-tung was born on 26 December 1893 in a small village in Hunan province. His father was a prosperous farmer and he paid for Mao to attend the village school. When he was thirteen, Mao was forced to leave school and begin work on the family farm. But he was determined to continue his education and in 1910–11 he left his family and went to study at a secondary school in the provincial capital of Changsha.

It was in Changsha that Mao first learned of the ideas of Sun Yat-sen and the Nationalists. During the Revolution of 1911 Mao spent six months as a soldier in the revolutionary army of Hunan. Afterwards he entered the Teachers' Training School in Changsha. On graduating in 1918 he became an assistant librarian in Peking University. At this time he first began to study the writings of Karl Marx and the events of the Communist Revolution in Russia. Eventually he became a convinced Communist.

During the 1920s Mao became an important figure in the newly founded Chinese Communist Party. He began forming Communist groups amongst the miners and industrial workers in Hunan. In September, 1922, Mao helped to organise strikes in protest against working conditions in factories and mines. The strikes failed. When Mao's arrest was ordered, he was forced to escape with his wife and children to the coastal city of Shanghai.

In 1926 when Mao became head of the peasant department of the CCP, he returned to Hunan. He spent nine months touring the province and investigating the problems of the peasants. Every year taxes were increased to pay for the army of the local Warlords. These soldiers trampled the crops and stole animals. Landlords demanded higher rents. Year by year more peasants were forced to leave their homes, and so become unemployed.

Mao was very concerned about the hardships of the peasants and he began to form peasants' associations. In September 1927, he led them in the Autumn Harvest Uprisings against the landowners. The revolt failed because there were few leaders and the peasants were poorly armed. Once again Mao was forced to flee for his life while the landlords took their revenge on the rebels.

The uprising and his work amongst the peasants had a great influence on Mao. Before his year in Hunan, Mao believed that the industrial workers in the towns would be "the leading force in our [Communist] revolution". Afterwards he realised that no revolution would be successful without the support of the peasants who formed 90 per cent of the population of China. The peasants had serious grievances which could only be solved by destroying the power of the landlords and the Warlords in the countryside. If they were to do this, the peasants must be armed, educated in Communist ideas and trained in guerrilla warfare.

Mao's ideas were strongly opposed by the majority of the Communist Party and Mao was dismissed from the Politburo. This could have been the end of his political career. Instead, he decided to return to the countryside and continue with his work of organising and training the peasants. By 1929 Mao had collected an army of over 11 000 men in the mountains of the borders of Hunan and Kiangsi provinces. This became known as 'the Red Army'.

2 THE LONG MARCH

The escape from the Kiangsi Soviet base

In October 1934 Mao and the main body of the Red Army fled from their Kiangsi Soviet base to escape certain annihilation by the KMT forces. 100 000 soldiers and officials, carrying personal belongings, weapons, money and other equipment, set out to reach another base at Sangchih in North West Hunan. The enemy Kuomintang (KMT) troops were weakest to the west. The main body of the Red Army broke through in that direction, escaped from the encircling KMT Army and crossed the Hsiang River. But losses were heavy and there was growing criticism of the military leadership of Po Ku.

Chiang Kai-shek had blocked the road to Sangchih and so the Red Army now headed for North Szechuan. After crossing the Hsiang River they were faced by a mountain range, known as Laoshan (Old Mountain) which was:

so steep that I could see the sole of the man ahead of me. Steps had been carved out of the stone face of the mountain, they were as high as a man's waist . . . Next morning my group finally reached the sheer cliff, dei kungyai [Thunder God Rock], a solid cliff of stone jutting into the sky at about a ninety degree angle.

Stone steps no more than a foot wide had been carved up its face and up this we had to go without anything to hold on to. Horses with broken legs lay about the foot of the cliff.

(from Agnes Smedley, *The Great Road,* Monthly Review Press, 1956, pp. 313–4)

The capture of Tsunyi

Some men were sacrificed to cover the main retreat and the Red Army then approached the town of Tsunyi. This was guarded by the fast flowing Wu River and by steep cliffs, so it offered some security from the pursuing KMT troops. The sixth Regiment was ordered to storm the town but they took it by trickery instead. They dressed in captured enemy uniforms and pretended that they were KMT

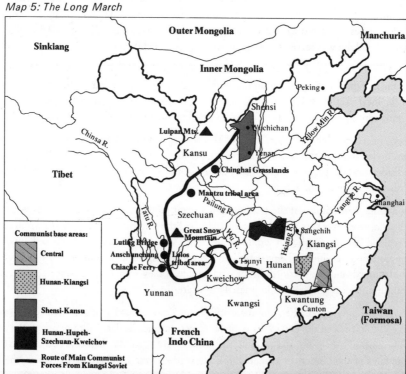

Map 5: The Long March

soldiers fleeing from the Communists. The garrison opened the gates of the town and, once inside, the Red Army troops overcame their resistance with very little fighting.

Mao and the Tsunyi Conference

Although by this time, the Red Army had lost about half its men, the capture of Tsunyi had given them freedom from immediate attack. While the men rested, Mao and the Communist leaders held a conference from 6th to 8th January. Mao supported by the generals, used the occasion to criticise Po Ku and to gain control in the Politburo. Mao was elected Chairman of the Military Committee of the Chinese Communist Party. Fourteen resolutions were passed and, in the final one, Mao sought to rally everyone to his leadership:

The Party has bravely exposed its own mistakes. It has educated itself through them and learnt how to lead the revolutionary war more efficiently towards victory. After the exposure of mistakes, the Party, instead of being weakened, actually becomes stronger.

(from Dick Wilson, *The Long March*, Hamish Hamilton 1971)

The building at Tsunyi where the Communists met in January 1935

The Chingkang Mountains: the Communists had to cross mountainous country like this during the Long March

The mountain pass outside Tsunyi

23

From this time on, Mao was the dominating personality in the Chinese Communist Party and he was to lead them to full control of China in 1949.

"Go north to fight the Japanese!"

The Conference also adopted the slogan "Go north to fight the Japanese". It was decided that they would try to link up with another section of the Red Army (known as the Fourth Front Army) which was then in Szechuan province. From here they would head for the Communist Soviet base in north Shensi province. From Shensi the Red Army could fight the Japanese in Inner Mongolia.

Mao and the main body of the Red Army resumed their Long March. Five weeks of heavy fighting followed as Chiang Kai-shek opposed Mao's attempts to cross the Yangtse River. The Red Army then turned south, aiming for the Chinsha (Golden Sands) River, with Chiang closely pursuing them.

The crossing of the Chinsha River

The Chinsha River falls by an average of 5.5 m per 1.8 km, which makes its current swift and navigation difficult. Crossing points were few and could easily be defended by the KMT. A regiment was sent to seize the Chiaoche crossing. After a forced march of a day and night, the regiment captured the ferry and routed reinforcements. The main army was able to cross in nine days and nights. By the time that the KMT found out what was happening, the Reds had burned the boats and were taunting them: 'Come on over, the swimming is fine!'

The Chihshui River and ferry in Kweichow province—another hazard which faced the Red Army on the Long March

A Lolos tribesman

The Lolos

Escape from one trap led straight into another. The Red Army was now boxed in by the Chinsha, Tatu and Min rivers and had to cross the Sikang Mountains. Here, there lived some non-Chinese people, the Lolos, who were hostile to all foreigners.

Shortly after we entered the Yi´ [Lolos] area, we saw thousands of people on the mountain slopes. They were brandishing home-made shot guns, spears and clubs . . . We were compelled to close our ranks and continue our march very cautiously in order to be prepared against a surprise attack. When we reached Kumatzu, a place about 30 li [about 16 km] inside the Yi area, our way was blocked by a big crowd of people and we were forced to stop.

(Dick Wilson)

However, the Red Army managed to gain the friendship of the Lolos. They bribed them with weapons and money, and one Red Army general drank the blood of a chicken to become a blood brother of the tribe.

The Tatu River

By the end of May they were approaching the Tatu River. One regiment marched to the Anshung-chang ferry, which was guarded by two companies of KMT soldiers. The speed of their advance took the defenders by surprise. Eighteen men volunteered for the assault party and, under covering fire, they took the opposite bank. The spring thaw was making the waters more turbulent and crossing the river became a slow and dangerous operation. The KMT air force appeared in strength and the Red Army was a sitting target for them. A new plan was needed.

The leaders met to consider the situation. At Luting, there was a suspension bridge that had been built in 1701. It was decided to try to force a crossing there. If that route failed, the Long March would be over.

In two days, over difficult country and in the face of determined KMT opposition, a Red Army regiment marched just over 161 km to Luting:

The mountains ahead rose in sheer cliffs. There was only a narrow path between them, climbing so sharply it was like a ladder to heaven. Your cap fell off when you tried to look all the way to the top. Forts had been built both on the mountain summits and at the head of the pass . . .

The rain pelted mercilessly; torrents rushed down the mountain gullies into the river. The twisting path along the side of the mountain had been difficult enough before; now the water made it as slick as oil . . . It was a case of every three steps a skid, every five steps a fall. We rolled rather than marched forward.

(Dick Wilson)

The Luting Bridge

The crossing of the Luting Bridge

Early in the morning of the third day, the Red Army reached the bridge and took up positions at the southern end.

It was not made of stone or of wood but of iron chains—13 in number, each big link as thick as a rice bowl. Two chains on each side served as railways: nine formed the surface walk.

(Dick Wilson)

Two KMT regiments lay in strong defensive positions at the northern end and the planks had been removed from the first half of the bridge. Yet there was no shortage of volunteers for the assault and, from among them, twenty-two were selected:

Platoon Commander Ma Ta-chin stepped out, grasped one of the chains, and began swinging, hand over hand towards the north bank. The platoon political director followed and, after him, the men. As they swung along, Red Army machine guns laid down a protecting screen of fire and the Engineering Corps began bringing up tree trunks and laying the bridge flooring. The army watched breathlessly as the men swung along the bridge chains. Ma Ta-chin was the first to be shot into the wild torrent below. Then another man and another. The others pushed along but just

25

before they reached the flooring at the north bridgehead they saw enemy soldiers dumping cans of kerosene on the planks and setting them on fire. Watching the sheet of flame spread, some men hesitated, but the platoon political leader at last sprang down on the flooring calling to the others to follow. They came and crouched on the planks releasing their hand grenades and unbuckling their swords.

They ran through the flames and threw their hand grenades in the midst of the enemy. More and more men followed, the flames lapping at their clothing. Behind them sounded the roar of their comrades, and beneath the roar the heavy THUD, THUD, THUD, of the last tree trunk falling into place. The bridge became a mass of running men with rifles ready, tramping out the flames as they ran.

(Agnes Smedley)

Fewer than fifty men were lost, although many were burned or wounded and, in two hours, the garrison defending Luting was defeated. Not long after, the troops who had managed to cross at Anshungchang arrived at Luting to rejoin the main body. The trap was broken and the Red Army could continue its march north.

Crossing the Snow Mountains

The Great Snow Mountain

Their aim was to link up with the Fourth Front Army in North Szechuan. That was less than 160 km away but seven mountain ranges had to be crossed first. The first was the Great Snow Mountain, 4 800 m high and, even in June, many of the poorly clad southerners died of exposure.

Chiachinsan (Great Snow Mountain) is blanketed in eternal snow. There are great glaciers in its chasms and every thing is white and silent . . .

Heavy fogs swirled about us, there was a high wind, and halfway up it began to rain. As we climbed higher and higher we were caught in a terrible hailstorm and the air became so thin we could hardly breathe. Speech was completely im-possible and the cold so dreadful that our breath froze and our hands and lips turned blue. Men and animals staggered and fell into chasms and disappeared for ever. Those who sat down to rest or to relieve themselves froze to death on the spot.

(Agnes Smedley)

Even in the mountains, the Communists were harassed by hostile tribes. Then, when they were over the mountains, they were further delayed when the rope suspension bridges over the Black Water River were destroyed.

The old Mekong suspension bridge

The meeting with the Fourth Front Army

The Fourth Front Army arrived in Moukung just before Mao and the main body of the Red Army. It had been forced out of its bases by increased KMT activity in North Szechuan. This meant the end of the Communist plan to set up a soviet there and, since the KMT was approaching from the north as well as the east, a new goal had to be chosen.

In the meetings that followed, disagreement flared up. Chang Kuo-tao, the Commander of the Fourth Front Army, wanted to occupy the Sikang-Western Szechuan regions or to retreat to Sinkiang. Mao, on the other hand, wanted to march north to Chinghai or to Outer Mongolia if necessary.

Chang spoke about his experience in Szechuan and claimed that his army was superior to Mao's. Mao, however, had the majority of support in the Politburo and the decision was made in his favour. The march north was to be continued.

The Chinghai grasslands

The Chinghai grasslands are situated on a plateau between 1 800 m and 2 700 m above sea level. It rains there for eight or nine months in the year and, because the drainage is bad, the land is marshy:

Huge clumps of grass grew on dead clumps beneath them . . . No tree or shrub grew here, no bird ventured near, no insect sounded. There was not even a stone. There was nothing, nothing but endless stretches of grass . . .

(Agnes Smedley)

Yet, because the KMT pursued them so closely, as Mao explained:

If we turn south it means running away, and the end of the revolution. We have no choice but to go forward.

(Dick Wilson)

A vanguard unit was sent ahead to blaze the trail, aided by a local guide, but the grasslands proved treacherous and took a heavy toll of men:

The water underfoot looked like horses' urine and gave off a smell which made people vomit . . .

and mosquitoes like horse leeches bit until:

Our faces went as black as a Negro's and our bodies became weaker and weaker . . .

Between the clumps the soil was exceptionally soft and loose, and if you took a step you would sink down at least 18 inches. Sometimes there were bottomless pools of mud. If you weren't careful, and took a false step, a man and his horse would sink down; the more they would struggle, the deeper they would go and if no one pulled them out that was the end of them.

(Dick Wilson)

Crossing the grasslands

The Mantzu Tribe

Food was short and they had to eat wild grass, roots and plants. Gathering food proved difficult because of the Mantzu tribes. The Mantzu Queen threatened to boil alive anyone who helped the Red Army soldiers. No wonder that when the survivors emerged from the swamps and returned to Chinese lands, one of them reported that the local peasants:

thought we were crazy. We touched their houses and the earth, we embraced them and we danced and sang and cried.

(Agnes Smedley)

An aerial view of Yenan, which the Communists decided to make the new Communist headquarters

Mao talks happily with peasants in Yenan

The end of the Long March

Another battle was fought at the Latzu Pass. Then followed the crossing of the Pailung River, the climbing of the Liupan Mountains and, finally, on 20 October 1935, the marchers met troops from the Shensi Soviet at Wuchichen. The Long March was over.

Mao led a party to the Soviet HQ and was greeted with banners:

Welcome Chairman Mao
Welcome to Central Red Army
Expand the Shensi-Kansu-Ninghsia
  soviet area !

Smash the enemy's third encirclement
  campaign !
Long live the Chinese Communist Party !
                 (Dick Wilson)

Mao in his cave dwelling in Yenan

Of the 100 000 soldiers and officials who had set out from Kiangsi in October 1934, only about 5000 survived the march. But Chiang Kai-shek had failed to destroy the Communists.

The Long March is a wonderful story of heroism and endurance. It enabled Mao Tse-tung to establish his leadership. The tactics that the Red Army developed showed how a guerrilla force could defeat a better armed and bigger army. The Long March also began the partnership between the Red Army and the peasants that was to play such an important part in the eventual triumph of the Communists.

THE IMPORTANCE OF THE LONG MARCH

In December 1935 Mao made a speech in which he gave his view of the Long March, and its importance in the history of the Communist revolution in China.

We say that the Long March is the first of its kind ever recorded in history . . . For twelve months we were under daily reconnaissance and bombing from the air by scores of planes. We were encircled, pursued, obstructed and intercepted on the ground by a big force of several hundred thousand men. We encountered untold difficulties and great obstacles on the way, but by keeping our two feet going we swept across a distance of more than 20,000 li through the length and breadth of eleven provinces.

Well, has there ever been in history a long march like ours? No, never. The Long March is also a manifesto. It proclaims to the world that the Red Army is an army of heroes and that the imperialists and their jackals, Chiang Kai-shek and his like, are perfect nonentities.

The Long March is also an agitation corps. It declares to the two hundred million people of eleven provinces that only the road of the Red Army leads to their liberation. Without the Long March, how could the broad masses have known so quickly that there are such great ideas in the world as are upheld by the Red Army? The Long March is also a seeding-machine. It has sown many seeds in eleven provinces, which will sprout, grow leaves, blossom into flowers, bear fruit and yield a crop in future. To sum up, the Long March ended with our victory and the enemy's defeat.

(from *The Selected Works of Mao Tse-tung*, Vol.I)

Mao with Chou En-lai during the Long March

3 WHY AND HOW DID THE COMMUNISTS TRIUMPH?

THE JAPANESE THREAT

By 1936, there were signs that Japan was planning a full-scale invasion of China. Mao Tse-tung urged the Kuomintang to join him in a united front against the invaders (Source 10).

Chiang Kai-shek was afraid, however, that his army would be so weakened in the fight against the Japanese that the way would be clear for the Communists to seize power. He decided that his first task must be to destroy the Red Army. Only then would he turn his attention to the task of driving the Japanese out of China.

He sent a force to attack the Red Army in their stronghold in Shensi province, but reports soon began to reach him that his troops were refusing to fight. Their commander, Chang Hsueh-liang, the 'Young Marshall', had been persuaded by the Communists to join forces with them against the Japanese.

Source 10

MAO TSE-TUNG URGES CHIANG KAI-SHEK TO JOIN HIM IN THE FIGHT AGAINST JAPAN

The Revolutionary Military Committee of the Red Army hereby solemnly advises the gentlemen of the Nanking government that at this critical moment of the threat of immediate destruction to the nation and the people, you ought, in all reason, to break with your past and, in the spirit of the maxim, 'Brothers quarrelling at home will join forces against attacks from the outside', to stop the nation-wide civil war . . . If, however, you obstinately refuse to awaken to reason, then your rule will certainly collapse in the end.

(*Selected Works of Mao Tse-tung*, Foreign Language Press, 1967)

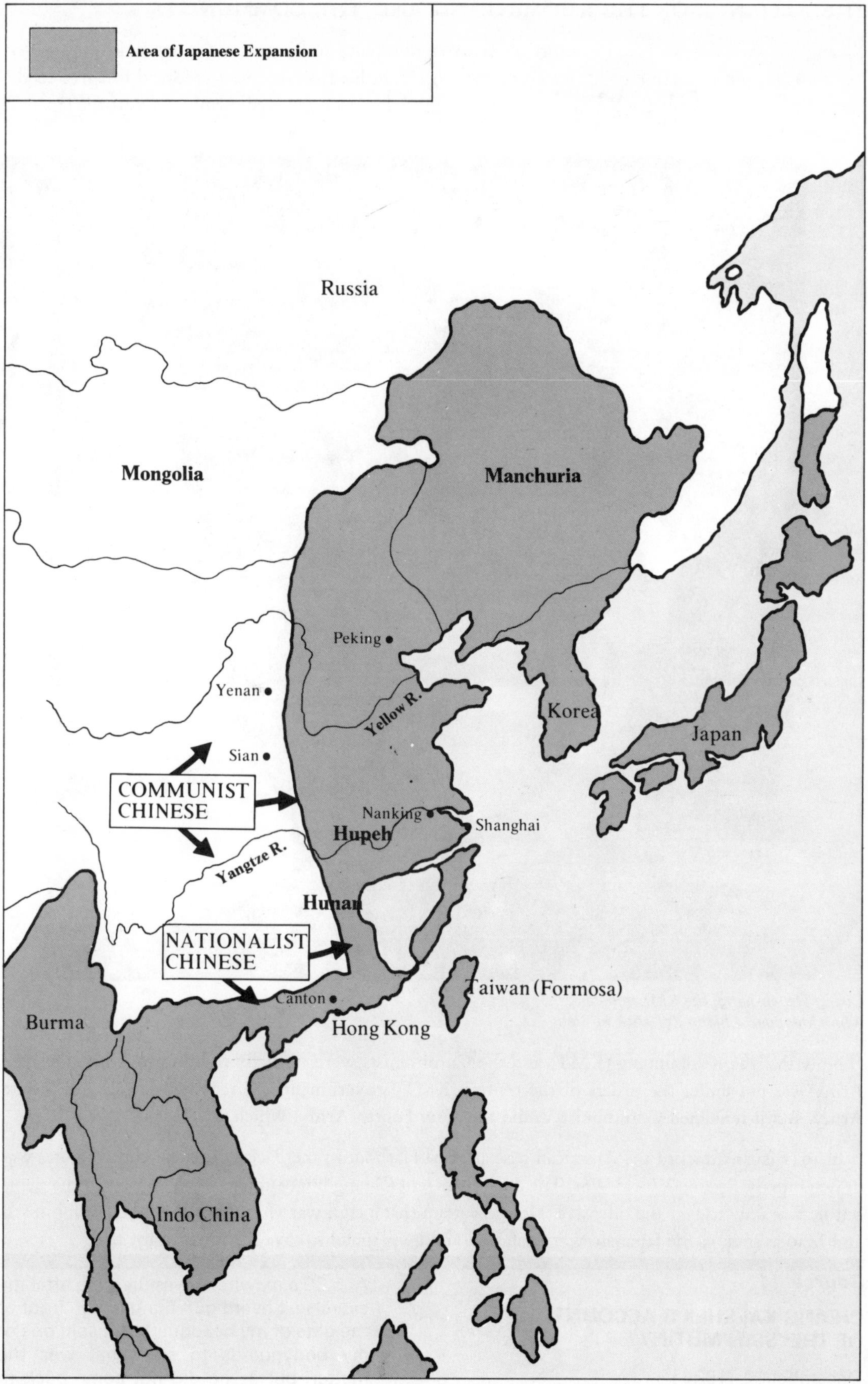

Area of Japanese Expansion
Russia
Mongolia
Manchuria
Peking
Yenan
Sian
Yellow R.
Korea
Japan
COMMUNIST CHINESE
Nanking
Shanghai
Hupeh
Yangtze R.
Hunan
NATIONALIST CHINESE
Canton
Taiwan (Formosa)
Hong Kong
Burma
Indo China

Map 6: Japanese expansion, 1937–1945

THE ALLIANCE OF THE KUOMINTANG AND THE COMMUNISTS

Chiang Kai-shek flew to Sian to restore his army to obedience to his orders. On his arrival, however, he was kidnapped by some of his own officers. To regain his freedom he was forced to agree to the Communist demand that the Kuomintang should fight alongside the Red Army to defeat the Japanese invaders (Sources 11, 12).

Chang Hsueh-liang, the KMT general
who kidnapped Chiang Kai-shek in Sian

Now that the Kuomintang (KMT) and the Communists were officially fighting together, the Red Army was put under the orders of the central (KMT) government and renamed the Eighth Route Army. But it remained Communist, as did the New Fourth Army, which was formed a year later.

In 1941 Japan attacked the American base at Pearl Harbour in the Pacific, and the United States was drawn into the Second World War. The Americans sent Chiang huge supplies of money and armaments but he was slow to take the offensive. He was certain that a civil war would break out between himself and Mao as soon as the Japanese were defeated and he planned to save his strength for that.

Source 11

CHIANG KAI-SHEK'S ACCOUNT OF THE 'SIAN MUTINY'

December 12 [1936]

At 5.30 a.m. when I was dressing after my exercise, I heard gun firing just in front of the gate of my headquarters. I sent one of my bodyguards to see what was the matter, but as he did not come back to report, I sent two others out and then heard gun firing again, which then continued incessantly . . .

Accompanied by Tso Pei-chi, one of my own guard officers, and Chiang Hsiao-chung, an A.D.C., I started for the mountain at the back of the house. After crossing the Fei Hung Bridge we found the eastern side door securely locked, and the key could nowhere be found. We then scaled the wall, which was only about ten feet high and not difficult to get over. But just outside the wall there was a deep moat, the bottom of which was about thirty feet [9 m] below the top of the wall. As it was still dark, I missed my footing and fell into the moat. I felt a bad pain and was unable to rise. About three minutes later I managed to stand up and walked with difficulty. After having walked several tens of paces we reached a small temple, where some of my bodyguards were on duty. They helped me to climb the mountain.

After about half an hour we reached the mountain top. Presently gun firing was heard on all sides. Bullets whizzed by quite close to my body. Some of the bodyguards were hit and dropped dead. I then realised that I was surrounded, that the mutiny was not local and that the whole of the North-eastern troops took part in it. So I decided not to take shelter but to go back to my headquarters and see what could be done. I walked down the mountain as quickly as I could. Halfway down the mountain I fell into a cave which was overgrown with thorny shrubs and in which there was barely enough space to admit me. I felt exhausted. Twice I struggled to my feet but fell down again. I was compelled to remain there for a rest and to wait further developments.

As the day gradually dawned I could see from the cave that the Lishan Mountain was surrounded by a large number of troops. Then I heard the detonation of machine guns and hand grenades near my headquarters. I knew that my faithful bodyguards at the headquarters continued their resistance and that the rebels were using artillery to attack them.

About twenty or thirty feet [6 or 9 m] from my refuge I heard someone hotly arguing with the rebels. It was Chiang Hsiao-chung's voice. The rebels made a more thorough search. I heard one of the mutinous soldiers above the cave saying: 'Here is a man in civilian dress, probably he is the generalissimo'.

Another soldier said: 'Let us first fire a shot'.

Still another said: 'Don't do that'.

I then raised my voice and said: 'I am the generalissimo. Don't be disrespectful. If you regard me as your prisoner, kill me, but don't subject me to indignities.'

The mutineers said: 'We don't dare'. They fired three shots into the air and shouted: 'The generalissimo is here!' . . .

After changing my residence Chang came to see me . . . Since many people had participated in the matter he said everything had to be decided by them jointly. Besides, they had already sent out a circular telegram including eight proposals and I must agree to some of them so that the coup might not become meaningless. If, said he, no results whatever were achieved, the crowd would not agree to sending me back.

The so-called eight proposals were:
1. Re-organise the Nanking [i.e. KMT] government so that members of other parties and cliques might come in and help save the nation;
2. Stop all civil wars;
3. Release immediately the patriotic leaders who had been arrested in Shanghai;
4. Pardon all political offenders;
5. Guarantee the people's liberty of assembly;
6. Give a free hand to the people to carry out patriotic movements;
7. Carry out the Leader's will faithfully [i.e. Sun Yat-sen];
8. Call a National Salvation Conference immediately.

I strongly rebuked him . . . I said I had determined to sacrifice my life rather than sign any document under duress.
> (General and Madame Chiang Kai-shek, *A Fortnight in Sian*, Double-day, Doran and Company Inc, 1937, pp. 123–149)

Source 12

ANOTHER ACCOUNT OF THE CAPTURE OF CHIANG KAI-SHEK AT SIAN

On December 12th, 1936, Chiang Kai-shek was captured by two of his own officers whose wrath . . . had been aroused by his policy of carrying out attacks on the Communists but not resisting the Japanese invader. Taking place in the city of Sian this became known as the Sian Incident . . . The possibility of the country's total subjugation [to Japan] brought demands for resistance not only by workers, peasants and members of the petty bourgeoisie but also from a section of the ruling class.

Generals Chang and Yang had been impressed by the Communist Party's policy of a national united front against the Japanese and had signed a secret friendly agreement to refrain from attacking each other and to resist Japan. A cease-fire was in effect in some areas. The slogan 'Chinese should not fight Chinese' created a surge of patriotic feeling. On December 4th, Chiang gave them both an ultimatum—either they march against the Communists or they would be transferred . . . The two generals decided to resort to military action.

At 5 a.m. on December 12th a small group of their men reached [Chiang's hotel]. After a short tussle with the sentries, they broke into his room. It was empty, but the bedding was still warm. His clothes were strewn about . . . The men searched the hill behind the building. There, cowering behind a rock, they found Chiang, barefoot and shivering, clad only in his under trousers and a silk robe. They drove him to General Yang's residence where he was held for three days . . . The Communist Party was firmly against a civil war and wanted Nanking and Sian to make common desire to resist the Japanese . . . The Sian incident was a turning point in contemporary Chinese history. Mao Tse-tung analysed it. 'The KMT were forced to abandon their civil war policy and yield to the demands of the people. With the settlement, an internal co-operation under new circumstances took shape and a nationwide war against Japan started.

(from an article by Shen Po-chun, in *China Reconstructs,* a magazine produced by the China Welfare Institute, Peking, December 1962)

Red army guerrillas operating behind enemy lines, preparing rocks and boulders for an attack on the Japanese

THE TACTICS OF THE RED ARMY

Mao Tse-tung's soldiers were very active. They used against the Japanese the guerrilla tactics that they had learned in their campaign against the KMT during The Long March (Sources 13, 14).

As they cleared each district of the enemy, the Red Army immediately set about improving life for the peasants. Mao's soldiers were recruited from the peasants and they understood their grievances at first hand.

Few peasants owned the land that they farmed. Some of them had to pay as much as two thirds of the value of their crops as rent. From time to time, local Warlords would rob them of their harvest or conscript them into their bands. Most of them had to borrow money and could scarcely afford to pay off the interest, let alone clear the debt. As a result, they lived in a state of fear and poverty. They had good reason to hate their landlords, the moneylenders and the Warlords (Sources 15,16).

Traditionally in China armies had lived off the countryside and people had lived in fear of soldiers. However, Mao had trained his troops from the beginning to regard themselves as the defenders of the ordinary people. This meant that the soldiers should pay for their supplies and help the families who housed them. In the areas where the Red Army was strong, rich landlords were forced to give up all their land, except as much as they could till by their own labour. The rent paid by the peasants was reduced. Cooperatives were formed to help them market their produce. Schools were opened and medical clinics were started.

A section of the Communist army on duty on the Great Wall during the war against the Japanese

Peasants and soldiers set out together at dusk to attack the enemy

It was their co-operation with the peasants that enabled the soldiers of the Eighth Route Army to operate guerrilla tactics and disappear behind the Japanese lines. By the time the Japanese surrendered in 1945, the Communists had won control over a vast area of China. Equally important, wherever they had appeared they had earned the enthusiastic support of the peasants.

Source 13

PEN TEH-HUAI EXPLAINS THE TACTICS OF THE COMMUNIST PARTY

There are certain rules of tactics which must be followed if the newly developing partisan [i.e. Communist] army is to be successful. These we have learned from our long experience, and though they are variable, I believe that departures from them generally lead to extinction . . . successful partisan warfare demands these fundamentals; fearlessness, swiftness, intelligent planning, mobility, secrecy and suddenness and determination in action. Lacking any of these, it is difficult for partisans to win victories.

Finally, it is absolutely necessary for the partisans to win the support and participation of the peasant masses. If there is no movement of the armed peasantry, in fact, there is no partisan base, and the army cannot exist. Only by implanting itself deeply in the hearts of the people, only by fulfilling the demands of the masses can partisan warfare bring revolutionary victory . . .

But nothing, absolutely nothing, is more important than this—that the Red Army is a people's army, and has grown because the people helped us.

I remember the winter of 1928, when my forces in Hunan had dwindled to a little over two thousand men, and we were surrounded. The Kuomintang troops burned down all the houses in a surrounding area of about 300 li, seized all the food there, and then blockaded us. We had no cloth, we used bark to make short tunics, and we cut up the legs of our trousers to make shoes. Our hair grew long, we had no quarters, no lights, no salt. We were sick and half starved. The peasants were no better off, and we would not touch what little they had.

But the peasants encouraged us. They dug up from the ground the grain which they had hidden from the White troops, and gave it to us, and they ate potatoes and wild roots. They hated the Whites for burning their homes and stealing their food. Even before we arrived they had fought the landlords and tax-collectors, so they welcomed us. Many joined us, and nearly all helped us in some way. They wanted us to win! And because of that we fought on and broke the blockade.

(Edgar Snow, *Red Star Over China*, Victor Gollancz, 1969, pp. 285–9)

Source 14

GUERRILLA OPERATIONS AGAINST THE JAPANESE

In Autumn 1941 the Japanese invaders occupied our country towns. Jan village fell under their heels. Wherever the Japanese went they massacred and looted. Almost every family dug holes something like vegetable cellars, to hide in. We called these 'frogholes'. In 1942 the Japanese started a mop-up campaign in central Hopei with their 'burn all, kill all, loot all' policy . . . They set up three fortified strongholds and twelve pillboxes within a radius of fifteen kilometres from our village and harassed us every two or three days. Soon they discovered our 'frogholes'.

One day they seized ten of our people and killed five of them . . . How could we keep ourselves from being looted and killed and at the same time strike at the enemy? . . . We decided to open two or more entrances to each of our 'frogholes' so that if the enemy discovered one entrance we could get away through others. Then we began to dig tunnels to link the holes together. The whole village pitched in. We worked in the day and dug tunnels at night. By the beginning of 1945 we had completed four main tunnels with twenty-four branches radiating out from them. We also dug more than fifteen kilometres of tunnels to connect us with neighbouring villages.

(*China Reconstructs*, November 1970)

The people of Chung King emerging from caves which served as air raid shelters, 1942

Source 15

CONDITIONS OF PEASANT LIFE BEFORE THE COMMUNISTS CAME TO POWER

Many peasants took up tobacco cultivation, not primarily because of the expected returns but rather because, in the midst of their poverty, tobacco planting was the only way to obtain seed and loans.

The growth of tobacco from seedling to harvest takes about ninety days, from May to the middle of August. After harvesting the leaves are baked in an underground house kept at a definite temperature. This is a bare house of about eight feet square [2.5 m], without light. It is thickly hung with tobacco leaves which are usually looked after by a woman, who stays there throughout the baking process. If it were possible to look into such a house one would probably see a figure with dirty face and uncombed hair, wearing a pair of red trousers tied tightly just above her tiny feet. She had to watch the leaves for about a week, being most of the time on her feet, and all the time in the hot, moist atmosphere.

During the collection season, long processions of wheelbarrows and carts drawn by oxen or horses move slowly along the winding, bumpy and dusty roads. The transportation of tobacco leaves to the market is made more difficult by the wind which frequently rises, carrying with it the thick, yellow dust which makes the way hard to find. At other times, sudden storms reduce the roads to thick mud which makes it hard for wheels to move, and huge pools form through which the peasants have to wade.

Arriving at the leaf collection ground, the peasants have to line up in one of the many queues, some of which are as long as two thirds of a mile [about one kilometre]. Confusion seems unavoidable and the police beat them into line with thonged whips. Exposed to hunger and cold they have to wait with the utmost patience, and those standing at the ends of the queues often have to wait for twenty-four hours and even then are unable to push through the crowd to the doors. Every year there are tragic incidents; some get trampled down by the crowd, some are fatally injured, being rammed by the shafts of the carts, and occasionally boys who are too young to hold their own in the crowd get smothered.

The collection house resembles a big barn with rows of wooden counters covered with bamboo stretchers upon which the peasants have to dump their leaves. Being afraid that the leaves will dry up and lose their lustre in the long interval before the inspector comes round, the peasants often take off their coats, in spite of the cold and use them to cover the leaves. They stand there with outstretched necks and tense expressions, eagerly awaiting the inspector who, in their minds, is the pronouncer of the final verdict of fortune or doom for the following twelve months. When the inspector finally arrives he quickly classifies the leaves by inspecting a few bunches, but if the peasant should hesitate to sell any one grade or any one stretcherful, all his leaves will be refused. Sometimes when the inspector finds several bunches of lower-grade leaves among those of a higher grade, he will confiscate the leaves as a warning. Should the peasant make any verbal protest, he gets roughly handled, and should he resist this

Another side of peasant life: peasants working a chain pump to irrigate the crops using water from the Han River

actively, the police are immediately called in to arrest him on charges of theft or disturbance of the peace. The peasant is invariably blamed for starting any such affair and in addition to possible fine and imprisonment he is severely cautioned at the time of release.

(Hsu Yung-sui article translated in *Agrarian China*, 1939)

Famine victims in Hunan province in front of their home which is little more than a hole in the ground

---

Source 16

ANOTHER DESCRIPTION OF CHINESE PEASANT CONDITIONS IN THE PAST

When times were good they ate millet and maize, with peppers, cabbage, marrows, and onions for flavour. Meat and eggs were rare indeed. When times were bad— and during wars they were always bad— there was not enough to eat. They then ate Kao-liang [a very course grain used for feeding animals], buckwheat and sweet potatoes. The army had compiled a handbook of famine foods, including wild jujubes, black dates, herb roots, tree leaves, fuller's earth, bark and various weeds.

(R. & N. Lapwood, *Through the Chinese Revolution*, Spalding and Levy 1954, p. 29)

CIVIL WAR BETWEEN THE KMT AND THE COMMUNISTS

In nine years of warfare against Japan, China had suffered severely. Mao Tse-tung was anxious, therefore, to prevent any more fighting from breaking out between the Red Army and the Kuomintang. In August 1945, he asked Chiang Kai-shek to meet him to see whether they could find some peaceful solution to the problem of governing China.

The Americans also were eager to persuade Chiang not to renew the civil war and sent one of their most respected soldiers, General Marshall, to advise him. Peace was maintained for almost a year, but by the summer of 1946 Chiang had begun his campaign to wipe out the Communists and General Marshall had to acknowledge that his mission had failed.

Chiang was confident that he could crush the opposition quickly. He had an army of about three million men, compared with the Communists' one million, and he could rely on almost unlimited supplies of money and military equipment from America. There seemed to be good reason for his optimism (Source 17). Yet within three years he suffered a crushing defeat.

Source 17

A FOREIGN VIEW OF COMMUNIST 'WEAKNESS' IN 1945

The nature and the scope of the dissolution in North China, however, was at this time well concealed from the general public in the Yangtze Valley. The ignorance of people about events that were transpiring in Communist areas surprised me. When I told foreign officials that an offensive had begun, they looked at me as if I were crazy. 'Forget it', said one high-ranking army officer, 'The Communists have no weapons and will never be able to launch an offensive'. A member of a foreign embassy . . . told me my statement that the peasants were joining One-Eyed Liu against Nanking was a lot of Communist 'crap'. What did the peasants care about the war? . . . These men would not expose their minds to the shock of revolution.

(Jack Belden, *China Shakes the World,* Victor Gollancz, 1950, p. 169)

THE DEFEAT OF CHIANG KAI-SHEK AND THE KMT

By June 1948 the size of the two armies was about equal and at the end of that year Mao's troops forced an important section of the Nationalist Army to surrender. Although the Nationalists were better equipped in 1946, it is not altogether surprising that the Communists defeated them.

The Red Army was better led. Unlike Chiang, Mao Tse-tung left his field commanders free to fight their battles without interference from him. Many of Chiang's leading advisers were corrupt and used the civil war to make themselves wealthy. Much of the aid that came from America to help the Kuomintang in the fight against the Communists went into their pockets. The peasants had learned

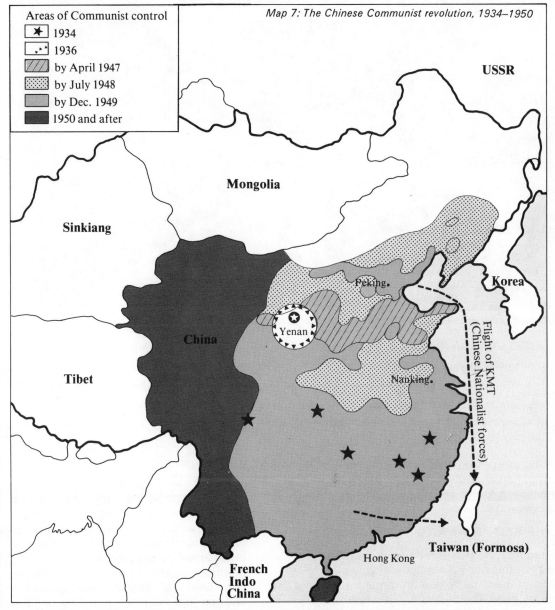

Map 7: The Chinese Communist revolution, 1934–1950

Areas of Communist control
- ★ 1934
- 1936
- /// by April 1947
- by July 1948
- by Dec. 1949
- 1950 and after

USSR

Mongolia

Sinkiang

Peking.

Korea

Yenan

China

Nanking.

Tibet

Flight of KMT (Chinese Nationalist forces)

Taiwan (Formosa)

Hong Kong

French Indo China

from experience that they could expect no improvement in their conditions under Chiang, whereas under the Communists, they were better off than they had ever been. The result was that the Red Army had the enthusiastic support of the peasants wherever they appeared (Source 18).

Peasants assisting the Red Army to sabotage Japanese transport

The Nationalists (KMT supporters) who had been wealthy at the beginning of the war found that by 1948 their money was worthless; prices had risen 85 000 times in six months!

The Kuomintang soldiers had no stomach for a fight in which they were badly led and which brought them into conflict with the peasants. They surrendered in droves, complete with their equipment, to the Communists. The arms and munitions that America had sent to support the Kuomintang were the ones that carried the Red Army to victory.

In January 1949, Peking surrendered without a struggle and in October of the same year Canton fell. The civil war was over and the People's Republic of China was proclaimed (Source 19).

Source 18

THE RED ARMY AND THE MASSES

Gradually the Red Army's work with the masses improved, discipline strengthened, and a new technique in organisation developed. The peasantry everywhere began to volunteer to help the revolution. As early as Chingkanshan the Red Army had imposed three simple rules of discipline upon its fighters, and these were prompt obedience to orders; no confiscations whatever from the poor peasantry, and prompt surrender directly to the

Government, for its disposal, of all goods confiscated from the landlords. After the 1928 Conference emphatic efforts to enlist the support of the peasantry were made, and the following rules were drawn up:

1. Replace all doors when you leave a house;
2. Return and roll up the straw matting on which you sleep;
3. Be courteous and polite to the people and help them when you can;
4. Return all borrowed articles;
5. Replace all damaged articles;
6. Be honest in all transactions with the peasants;
7. Pay for all articles purchased;
8. Be sanitary, and especially establish latrines a safe distance from people's houses.

(Edgar Snow, *Red Star Over China*)

Red Army soldiers with captured KMT equipment: notice the American armoured vehicles in the background

Source 19

THE PEOPLE'S REPUBLIC OF CHINA IS PROCLAIMED

Our work will be written down in the history of mankind, and it will clearly demonstrate the fact that the Chinese who comprise one quarter of humanity, have from now on stood up . . . We have united ourselves and defeated both our foreign and domestic oppressors by means of the People's War of Liberation and the people's great revolution, and we announce the establishment of the People's Republic of China. Our nation will from now on enter the large family of peace-loving and freedom-loving nations of the world. It will work bravely and industriously to create its own civilisation and happiness and will, at the same time, promote world peace and freedom. Our nation will never again be an insulted nation. We have stood up.

(Quoted in Myra Roper, *China in Revolution 1911–1949*, Edward Arnold, 1971)

Red Army victory parade through Shanghai: notice the American helmets captured from the KMT

Chairman Mao proclaims the Chinese People's Republic

4 MAO'S CHINA: REBUILDING A NATION

PLANS AND TARGETS

On 1 October 1949 from the top of the Gate of Heavenly Peace in Peking, Mao Tse-tung, Chou En-lai and other Communist leaders watched a great procession of Red Army soldiers, peasant fighters and other party workers go past in a triumphal march. Mao had just announced the foundation of the People's Republic of China. It was a day of great rejoicing.

A few months earlier Mao had talked to his fellow-Communists about their success:

Twenty eight years of our Party are a long period, in which we have accomplished only one thing—we have won basic victory in the revolutionary war. This calls for celebration, because it is the people's victory, because it is a victory in a country as large as China.

But he had gone on to sound a warning:

We still have much work to do; to use the analogy of a journey, our past work is only the first step, in a long march of ten thousand li. Remnants of the enemy have yet to be wiped out. The serious task of economic construction lies before us. We shall soon put aside some of the things we know well and be compelled to do things we don't know well. This means difficulties.

Peasant refugees from the fighting

When the Communists came to power in 1949, China was in a state of chaos. The countryside and the towns were both badly scarred, not only by the recent civil war, but by a century of continual fighting. Mao Tse-tung taught the people that they could recover from this disastrous condition and develop their great wealth if they regarded 'agriculture as the foundation and industry as the leading factor'.

The remains of a factory destroyed by Japanese bombardment

Taking 'agriculture as the foundation' meant that China must produce enough rice and grain, as well as wool and cotton, to feed and clothe everyone in the country. Regarding 'industry as the leading factor' meant that she had to produce the machines that would make her farming efficient and also manufacture the goods that would make the whole country wealthy and powerful. The two must advance hand in hand.

A starving refugee gnaws the bark of a tree

LAND REFORM

The first task was to deal with the problem of the landlords. As far back as the 1920s, during the civil war with the Kuomintang, wherever the Red Army had won control of an area, they had seized the land from the wealthy landlords and shared it among the peasants (Source 20).

In 1950, the Government extended this policy throughout the whole country by passing the Agrarian Reform Law. To make sure that this law was properly carried into effect, cadres were sent to all parts of China. In each village, they showed the inhabitants how to form themselves into a Peasant Association

43

and taught them to 'stand up' to the men who had oppressed them in the past. Landowners were summoned to appear before People's Courts to answer for their evil deeds and some estimates say that as many as one million were executed for their crimes (Source 21).

In the share-out of land, most families received no more than about one quarter-hectare. On such small holdings they were able to produce only enough to feed themselves, so they were encouraged to form cooperatives. It was hoped that by sharing their labour and their tools they would produce a surplus of food to send to the towns to feed the industrial workers.

The trial of a landlord before a people's court in 1953

Source 20

DESTROYING THE LANDLORDS

I came from a peasant home . . . I began working when I was seven. I herded cows and goats until 1918, when I began working in the fields . . .

In 1927 a peasants' organisation was set up here and that was when I first heard of communism. 'Destroy the landowners and do away with taxes', was the cry . . . That year we refused to pay taxes.

In 1931, 1932 and 1933 I kept hearing how there were revolutionaries in Suiteh and Tsechang who had destroyed the landowners and done away with taxes. That made a deep impression on me. I especially liked the idea of the landowners being destroyed, because landowners lived in luxury, while the people suffered...

In 1935 . . . there was a lot of talk then about the Red Army. In April that year Liu Chih-tan sent a guerrilla group to Thirty-mile Village to wipe out an armed land-owner group. The Red Army's slogan was 'Down with the local landowners! Down with the local despots! Down with imperialism! Divide the land equally! Free the women! Abolish taxes!'

It was now my job to organise the people of the neighbouring villages. I had to find leaders who could help the Red Army and see that it was given food and information and was kept up to date with the landowners' plans. In the district there were two detachments of the landowners' armed forces Ming Tuan, and also a dozen or so police, so I had to work in secret. They used to cut off the head of any of us they happened to get hold of. When I went to a village, it was in disguise. Once there, I visited the poorest villagers, the farmhands and daily labourers, and talked with them. I spoke about the revolution with those I thought I could trust and gave them the job of giving the Red Army all the support it needed.

In the end, the landowners no longer dared stay in the villages at night, but made fortified places for themselves up on the hillside and withdrew to those. After I had organised twenty villages, one of the Ming Tuan detachments fled, but the other remained . . . We agreed that we would send a 'feather-letter' round the villages. This is a letter with a feather. As soon as it reaches one village, it is sent on to the next, and so everyone knows what is going to be done. By the next morning six hundred farmers had arrived, and we arranged a mass meeting and elected a revolutionary committee.

(Jan Myrdal, *Report from a Chinese Village*, Heinemann, 1964 p. 48)

Source 21

MAO TSE-TUNG EXPLAINS WHY THE PEASANTS REACTED SO STRONGLY AGAINST THE LANDLORDS

This is what some people call 'going too far', or 'exceeding the proper limits in righting a wrong', or 'really too much'.

Such talk may seem plausible, but in fact it is wrong. First, the local tyrants, evil gentry and lawless landlords have themselves driven the peasants to this. For ages they have used their power to tyrannise over the peasants and trample them underfoot, that is why the peasants have reacted so strongly.

The most violent revolts and the most serious disorders have invariably occurred in places where the local tyrants, evil gentry and lawless landlords perpetrated the worst outrages. The peasants are clear-sighted. Who is bad and who is not, who is the worst and who is not quite so vicious, who deserves severe punishment and who deserves to be let off lightly—the peasants keep clear accounts, and very seldom has the punishment exceeded the crime.

(Mao Tse-tung, *Selected Works*, Foreign Language Press, 1963)

FIVE-YEAR PLANS

By 1952, the country had recovered from the war damage well enough for a further big advance to become possible. A Five-Year Plan to boost the country's heavy industry ran from 1953 to 1957.

Encouraged by their success, the Government prepared a second Five-Year Plan. Mao Tse-tung's aim was that China should make a 'Great Leap Forward' and win a place among the leading industrial powers of the world by 'walking on two legs'. By this policy, he meant balancing her effort between agriculture and industry, between large-scale and small-scale industry, and between modern and old fashioned methods (Source 22).

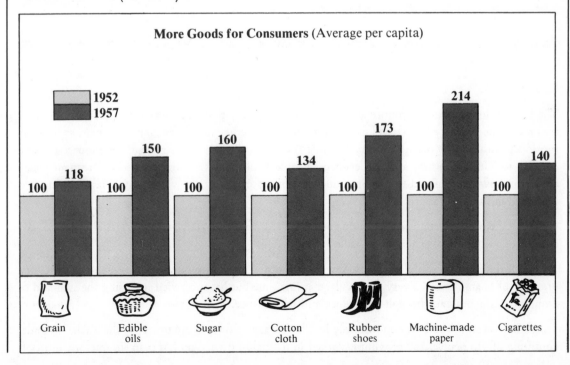

More Goods for Consumers (Average per capita)

1952
1957

	Grain	Edible oils	Sugar	Cotton cloth	Rubber shoes	Machine-made paper	Cigarettes
1952	100	100	100	100	100	100	100
1957	118	150	160	134	173	214	140

Source 22

THE FIRST YEAR OF THE SECOND FIVE-YEAR PLAN

The Chief Tasks of the Plan are:

To promote a new upsurge of agricultural production starting with a record harvest this year.

To further develop the heavy industries emphasising fuels, electric power and raw materials for large-scale expansion of plant and output, and chemical fertilisers and farm machinery to stimulate agriculture.

To promote and improve the people's living standards, culture, education and health.

(*China Reconstructs,* May 1958)

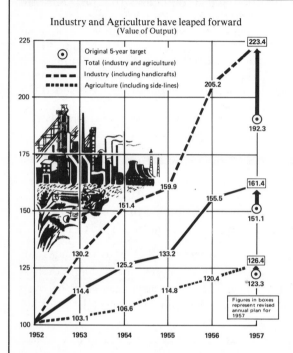

Industry and Agriculture have leaped forward
(Value of Output)

Original 5-year target
Total (industry and agriculture)
Industry (including handicrafts)
Agriculture (including side-lines)

Figures in boxes represent revised annual plan for 1957

Increase of Main Industrial and Farm Products			
	1952 output	1957 target	Increase %
Pig iron	1 900 000 tonnes	5 554 000 tonnes	192.3
Steel	1 349 000 tonnes	4 987 000 tonnes	269.8
Electric power	7 260 000 000 kwh	18 860 000 000 kwh	159.8
Coal	63 528 000 tonnes	117 271 000 tonnes	84.6
Crude oil	436 000 tonnes	1 500 000 tonnes	244.0
Ammonium sulphate	181 000 tonnes	499 000 tonnes	174.9
Cement	2 861 000 tonnes	6 807 000 tonnes	137.9
Machine tools	13 734	22 640	64.8
Cotton yarn	3 618 00 bales	4 635 000 bales	28.1
Cotton piece-goods	3848 000 000 metres	5018 000 000 metres	30.5
Machine-made paper	372 000 tonnes	836 000 tonnes	124.8
Sugar	451 000 tonnes	874 000 tonnes	93.8
Grain	154 400 000 tonnes	191 000 000 tonnes	23.7
Cotton	1 303 500 tonnes	1 500 000 tonnes	15.1

COMMUNES

The big development in agriculture at this time was the formation of communes. By 1957, in one or two areas, the peasant cooperatives had begun to join together into larger units. So marked was the improvement that they brought about that, in 1958, Mao called on the peasants throughout the whole country to 'Get organised', and he declared, 'People's communes are fine'. The Government issued advice on how to form and run a commune, and by 1959 almost the whole of China's farming was organised in this way (Source 23).

A typical commune consists of about 25 000 people divided into units, called brigades. Each brigade consists of a number of smaller units, called teams.

One of the most successful brigades is to be found in Tachai, a mountain area in the north China province of Shansi. It was a very poor village at one time but has succeeded in raising the standard of living of all the peasants through hard work and self-reliance.

Standards achieved still vary enormously in Chinese agriculture. In August 1975 the Tachai brigade, consisting of 550 people, 160 of whom worked in the fields, owned no less than six tractors, most of

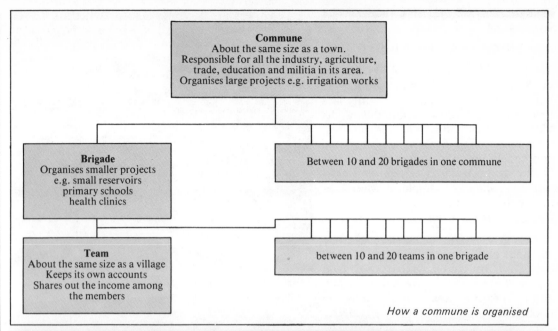

Commune
About the same size as a town.
Responsible for all the industry, agriculture,
trade, education and militia in its area.
Organises large projects e.g. irrigation works

Brigade
Organises smaller projects
e.g. small reservoirs
primary schools
health clinics

Between 10 and 20 brigades in one commune

Team
About the same size as a village
Keeps its own accounts
Shares out the income among
the members

between 10 and 20 teams in one brigade

How a commune is organised

Peasants in the Tachai Brigade begin to transform their poor village

them versatile caterpillar tractors. The neighbouring Nannao brigade in the same commune (admittedly with only 304 people) had only one hand tractor. Nannao could hire tractors from the commune, and the peasants were doing their best to equal the successes of nearby Tachai.

Mechanisation of agriculture and scientific methods of farming are the new goals which will increase production, and mechanised Tachai is the new model: in the words of the *People's Daily* (18 October, 1975): 'The mechanisation of agriculture must be by and large put into practice before 1980'.

47

SHASHIYU, 'VALLEY OF STONES'

Yen Lai-chiun is one of the 670 peasants in Shashiyu, a commune production brigade [village] in Tsunhua county less than 100 miles [160 km] from Peking. Its 130 families, including Yen, his wife and their two teenaged sons have sweated and strained over the years to build this 'Valley of Stones' into a farm area considered a shining example of Mao Tse-tung's thesis that people 'are the motive force' in making history.

Shashiyu is no paradise. By any standard of modern agriculture it is still backward. But the changes since Chiang Kai-shek's forces were driven out in 1947, and the peasants took over the land, are enormous.

At first, the village was heavily dependent on government aid—30,000 catties of grain a year, and almost 300 suits of padded clothes, the first few years. Today there is enough grain left over after a harvest to sell some to the state.

Winter and summer, visitors from all over China (like the 100 I met from Yunnan province far in the southwest) come here to see the changes wrought, how this parched land and these once barren hills have been turned into orchards and terraced fields of grain. They also come to take back with them the spirit of people who literally grew grain and fruit trees on rocks, carrying soil up slopes now terraced by rock-walls and afforested with pine and spruce.

The masses of the Hsipu Brigade build an irrigation channel in the year of the Great Leap Forward

Industry provides the machinery to modernise China's farming

Small scale industry: two girls from a commune production team making hoes and other simple agricultural implements

A peasant girl driving a tractor on a commune

Girls on a commune in Southern China use an electric husker to strip rice off stalks. Dry stalks are used for fuel or thatching

Tachai transformed by self-reliant peasants

I spent two days here with the Yen family. Lean and weather-beaten, Yen Lai-chiun wears a blue cap and the typical black-padded jacket and trousers of the northern countryside. The family lives in a 3-room stone dwelling—two rooms and, between them, a kitchen. There is a small backyard where corn is grown and pigs are raised; outdoor toilet facilities are enclosed by a shoulder high stone wall.

Farming in this part of China is at a standstill in winter. But there is much to do to get ready for spring planting. I accompanied Yen down the hill he lives on, to his winter work-place. We went through the flat part of Shashiyu which houses the primary school. It is open 35 weeks in the year and gives all 140 school-age children here a seven year course. There is also a small clinic housing a pharmacy where Chinese and Western medicines are made.

Yen took me into the one-room department store. Two young men worked behind the counter. The range of products was far less than in the cities, but the daily necessities were plentiful—dishes, enamelware, pots, toothbrushes and toothpaste. There were also some canned goods, local and out-of-province wines, fruit and the tasty walnuts grown here.

We headed for a rock-strewn hill. Others around it were terraced, pine and spruce covering some. We arrived at Yen's winter worksite where young men and women were burrowing a tunnel 250 metres through the hill to tap the water which flowed on the other side. Work had started last May and the job of tunnelling from both sides will be completed by Chinese New Year.

(Julian Schuman, *China's Changing Countryside*, 1972)

INDUSTRY

To meet the targets set for industry in the Great Leap Forward China needed much more steel. To back up the large-scale steel mills, people of all classes, from peasants to professors, were urged to build furnaces in their back-yards. As a result, more steel was made but, unfortunately, most of it was useless because the small furnaces could not get up enough heat. Many of the aims that had been set for the second Five-Year Plan had to be abandoned, though the Great Leap Forward was not regarded as a failure in China.

Since the Great Leap, China has undergone two more Five-Year Plans. Oil has become more important in the economy and China now produces enough for her own use and is able to export some. At Taching, in North East China, most of the agricultural work which was done by the men before the oil field was developed, is now done by the women. Equality for Chinese women has meant that they work as hard as the men in industry and in farming. It is regarded as very important in China that industry and agriculture should develop side by side (Source 24).

Despite set-backs from time to time, both in industry and in agriculture, there can be no doubt that life for the mass of the people has changed out of all recognition since the Communists came to power in 1949 (Source 25).

Large-scale industry: a modern oil refinery

Peasants help to build a steel mill

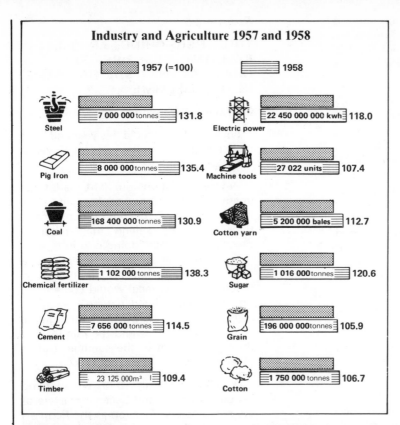

Industry and Agriculture 1957 and 1958

▨ 1957 (=100)　　　☰ 1958

Steel
7 000 000 tonnes — 131.8

Electric power
22 450 000 000 kwh — 118.0

Pig Iron
8 000 000 tonnes — 135.4

Machine tools
27 022 units — 107.4

Coal
168 400 000 tonnes — 130.9

Cotton yarn
5 200 000 bales — 112.7

Chemical fertilizer
1 102 000 tonnes — 138.3

Sugar
1 016 000 tonnes — 120.6

Cement
7 656 000 tonnes — 114.5

Grain
196 000 000 tonnes — 105.9

Timber
23 125 000 m³ — 109.4

Cotton
1 750 000 tonnes — 106.7

A model of an oil refinery at the Kwangchow Export Commodities Fair

Stamp commemorating the development of Chinese industry, 1949-59

Source 24

TSUNHUA'S INDUSTRY

My first stop in Tsunhua, less than 100 miles [160 km] northeast of Peking by rail and car, was a commune tractor station. In addition to ten tractors for 20 000 mu of farmland, Jianming commune's machines are used as bulldozers and for transporting rocks which abound in some parts of this hilly area. Repairs are done at the station, and, except for one vintage Czech caterpillar, all the tractors are made in China.

Jianming also has a farm machinery station where carts, tractors, pumps, motors, threshers and some diesel engines are repaired. What began in 1958 as a two-room shop is now seven workshops, including a small foundry for iron casting. The station turns out small pumps, 12-pound [about 5 kg] hammers made from melted down scrap steel—some hammers go on the market outside the county—and kettles. Apart from some old equipment bought from city factories, the station makes its own equipment—lathes, sheet cutters, electric saws.

Local industry in this county of 550 000 people consists of 110 factories, some with several hundred workers. Sixty-seven of these are located on Tsunhua's 44 communes.

Like Tsunhua, more than half the 200 counties in China, practising self-reliance and self-sufficiency, have similar small industries — plants making fertiliser, cement, machinery, iron and steel. Some also have small coal mines.

(Julian Schuman)

**More new things China
will make in 1958**

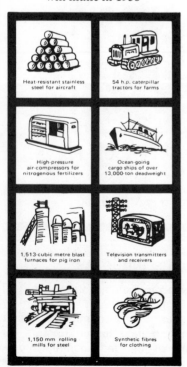

Heat-resistant stainless steel for aircraft

54 h.p. caterpillar tractors for farms

High-pressure air-compressors for nitrogenous fertilizers

Ocean-going cargo ships of over 13,000-ton deadweight

1,513-cubic metre blast furnaces for pig iron

Television transmitters and receivers

1,150 mm rolling mills for steel

Synthetic fibres for clothing

Source 25

TUNG HSIU-CHING, AN OLD RESIDENT, DESCRIBES THE CHANGES THAT SHE HAS SEEN IN HER LIFETIME

Our lane has changed.

I'm seventy years old this year and have been living in Nanyutai Lane for 33 years. What great changes I've seen!

Before liberation, our lane had three 'manys'—many poor people, many slum houses and many children. People made their living by selling their labour—pedalling pedicabs, doing odd jobs, running small stalls. None of them had a fixed job. Many families did not know where their next meal would come from. The houses they lived in were in a terrible state, with the wind whistling through the cracks in the winter and the rain leaking through the roof in the summer. But in those days who cared about us?

With liberation in 1949, we working people stood up and became masters of the new society. As soon as the People's Liberation Army men entered the city, they provided us with food, money and clothes. They got us together and explained the revolution to us. The people's government began solving the problem of

Nanyutai Lane, where Tung Hsiu-ching lives

unemployment and we all got steady jobs. Some went into factories and others joined producers' co-ops. With stable monthly wages, our life improved steadily.

Our people's government thinks of everything for us. More than 100 families in our lane have moved into new apartments or houses. The homes of the others have been well-repaired. The street's housing management office always asks for the opinions of the neighbourhood representatives before they distribute or renovate housing. If anything goes wrong with the electricity, water or drains, we just tell the office and it sends repairmen right away.

(*China Reconstructs,* August 1973)

5 MAKING AND KEEPING CHINA COMMUNIST

EARLY SUPPORT FOR THE CHINESE COMMUNIST PARTY

In 1949 when the People's Republic was set up, the Chinese Communist Party seemed to be supported by, or at least was not opposed by, the vast majority of working people in China. Although Marx had taught that industrial workers would bring about the revolution, Mao had shown that peasants could be revolutionaries too. As we have seen, much of his success was due to the way his Red Army had treated the peasants in the ten years or so before 1949.

But the new government in 1949 still had to solve the problem of establishing its control over a vast, sprawling nation of 600 million people. For the first few years they experienced little difficulty. The majority of the Chinese people were too busy working to repair the damage caused by the wars to question the authority of the Communist officials.

The Chinese Communist Party is not like a political party as we know them in Britain. It sees itself as an organisation which represents the interests of the majority of working people—peasants and factory workers. It admits that it suppresses the 'enemies of socialism'. These enemies are ex-landlords and businessmen who would like to see a return to a capitalist system in China. The vast majority of people in China supported the aims of Communism because it promised to improve their lives in many ways. Those who questioned the government were dealt with (Source 26).

Tableau forming part of a revolutionary exhibition in Canton: the wicked capitalist is brought to his knees and forced to read the works of Mao

'RAPID HOUSECLEANING' WHEN THE COMMUNISTS TOOK OVER

There was some rapid housecleaning when the Communists took over. The first victims were the obvious criminal elements and exploiters of the people . . .

Within three years of the Liberation the campaigns started. In 1951 was the First Campaign for the Suppression of Counter-revolutionaries. Every day brought dozens of public trials, and the people were encouraged to watch. Trials of People's Courts were broadcast over loudspeakers in public places, as the crowds shouted for death. The most to be shot in one day was 199, but in the countryside many, many more were put to knife, bullet and garrot. The fury of vengeance continued throughout March and April and then abated, as if out of breath.

(Bao Ruo-wang and Rudolph Chelminski, *Prisoner of Mao,* André Deutsch, 1975, p. 22)

A People's Court

THE FIRST SIGNS OF UNREST

In 1956, there were signs of unrest. This was sparked off by the action of the Soviet government in sending tanks and soldiers into Hungary to put down the rising there. Many Chinese intellectuals were afraid that their government was oppressing them in the same way that the Russian government was controlling the peoples of Eastern Europe. They demonstrated in the streets of large cities, such as Peking and Shanghai (Source 27).

Russian tanks invade Budapest during the Hungarian uprising, 1956

Mao Tse-tung was anxious to direct this criticism to constructive ends. In a speech, with a title based on an ancient Chinese saying, 'Let a hundred flowers blossom!', he urged that free discussion would help to determine what were the right policies to follow.

Source 27

DISTURBANCES IN CHINA FOLLOW THE HUNGARIAN RISING IN 1956

Certain people in our country were delighted when the Hungarian events took place. They hoped that something similar would happen in China, that thousands of people would demonstrate in the streets against the People's Government. Such hopes ran counter to the interests of the masses and therefore could not possibly get their support . . .

Many people refuse to admit that contradictions still exist in a capitalist society, with the result that when confronted with social contradictions they become timid and helpless . . . For this reason, we need to explain things to our people, our cadres in the first place, to help them understand contradictions in a socialist society and learn how to deal with such contradictions in a correct way.

(Mao Tse-tung *On the Correct Handling of Contradictions among the People* (February 1957), quoted in Winberg Chai (ed) *Essential Works of Chinese Communism*, Pica Press, 1970, pp. 332–3)

'LET A HUNDRED FLOWERS BLOSSOM!'

The flood of criticism was enormous, however, and Mao had to call a halt (Source 28). Many of the critics were forced to confess that they were 'poisonous weeds' rather than 'fragrant flowers'. They lost their positions in the Party and in the universities and were sent to corrective labour camps. The purpose of these labour camps was to 're-educate' those who were accused of working against the Communists, so that they should understand and accept the revolution. One person, who was held for seven years, was told when he was arrested:

In front of you are two paths: the one of confessing everything and obeying the government, which will lead you to a new life; the other of resisting the orders of the government and stubbornly remaining the people's enemy right to the very end. This path will lead to the worst possible consequences. It is up to you to make the choice. The sooner you confess your crimes, the sooner you will go home. The better your confession, the quicker you will rejoin your wife and children.

Mao the father figure, 1959

55

The Chinese see their present stage of development as one of Socialism. By this they mean that they are on the way to Communism, but inequalities still exist. Life in the city is better than life in the countryside. Different workers earn different wages. One commune is richer than another. Some people work mostly with their hands, others do mostly intellectual, or brain work. Women are still not with men. While these differences exist, they see it as important to struggle to narrow the gap between them.

Source 28

There is still debate as to whether the Hundred Flowers was an error on Mao's part or a coldly calculated ruse to make the regime's enemies speak up and thereby entrap themselves, but whatever the original planning, Mao reacted swiftly.

As of June, criticisms were no longer received as commentary, but rightist provocations. The Hundred Flowers was finished.
(Bao Ruo-wang and Rudolph Chelminski *Prisoner of Mao*, André Deutsch, 1975, pp. 25–26)

THE CULTURAL REVOLUTION

Up to the establishment of the People's Republic in 1949 and continuing until about 1960 the Party had followed Mao's ideas. His policies culminated in the Great Leap Forward when the communes were set up. Following the Great Leap, there were two years of terrible weather which led to bad harvests all over the country. The Soviet Union withdrew all its aid, technicians and plans for industry in 1960. Production figures for agriculture and industry fell and Mao's rivals began to argue against his ideas, wanting to put different policies into practice. During the 1960s in communes and factories and schools struggles were fought over these issues: should industry be developed in big units? should workers be paid according to how much they produced? should managers or workers decide plans for a factory? should private plots be enlarged in the communes? and so on.

Mao's view was that emphasis should be on collective work, that workers should take more part in decisions. Wages should not be determined by output; intellectual workers should take part in manual work and learn from the peasants. Most important, Mao believed that the Party should listen to the criticisms of the people. Mao saw that a new class of party officials, a group which considered itself superior, was growing up. If this was allowed to develop, China would not be continuing on the road to Communism.

Factory workers 'reporting new achievements'

THE RED GUARD MOVEMENT

Mao's concern about the future of China was no doubt one reason for his support of the Red Guards in 1966. But he may also have been worried about his own position. In the disappointment at the failure of the Great Leap Forward, Mao had for a while given up his position as Chairman to Liu Shao-chi (who was later denounced as a traitor), and since then he had not been secure as the single outstanding leader in China.

Mao smiles as Lui Shao-chi is elected Chairman of the People's Republic of China

Red Guard posters in Peking

A veteran soldier instructs young people in the revolutionary tradition

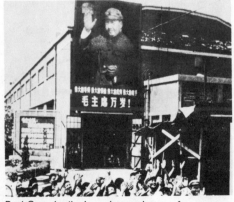

Red Guards display a huge picture of Chairman Mao over a quotation from his 'Thoughts'

In 1966, college and high school students throughout the country began a series of demonstrations against their teachers and people in authority. Something like a million and a half young people, from all parts of China, were invited to Peking to march past Mao.

This was the beginning of a great campaign to restore Mao to the position of undisputed leader of the Chinese people. The Red Guards denounced Mao's enemies in wall-posters and in great public demonstrations. They even made physical attacks on people and on their property. Millions of copies of the *Little Red Book* were distributed. This book contained a selection from the writing and speeches of Mao Tse-tung.

Red Guards re-naming the street on which the Soviet embassy is located

The 'May 7' cadre school in Shanghai, where people came to study the thoughts of Chairman Mao, learn a true revolutionary attitude and 'criticise the bourgeois world outlook'

In 1968 Mao disbanded the Red Guards. He decided that there was a danger that such young rebels would get out of hand. He gave the order for students and youthful intellectuals to be sent out into the countryside to work alongside the peasants and learn a true revolutionary attitude from them (Source 29).

Every means of propaganda was used to make Chairman Mao Tse-tung a figure of reverence. His portrait appeared on public hoardings and in the newspapers. Peasants, industrial workers and servicemen were persuaded that they could solve any problem and carry out their tasks better if they were to begin with a careful study of Mao Tse-tung thought.

Commune members studying quotations from Chairman Mao during a break from work

There is no area of life in China that has not gone through great changes as a result of the Cultural Revolution, but perhaps the changes were most marked in education. Education in China seems to mean the teaching of 'correct attitudes', that is training young people to accept and fight for Communism and serve the Communist state (Source 30). For this reason it is thought important that schooling should be closely linked to farming and factory work (Source 31).

Source 29

ACCOUNT BY A VILLAGER IN LIU LING OF THE CULTURAL REVOLUTION IN THE VILLAGE

There were a great many things I found wrong in the brigade. I read Mao Tse-tung and found people were not acting according to his ideas. But I didn't dare come out with my criticism. After all, I was only an ordinary member.

Not until the Red Guards arrived did things change. The Red Guards came to spread Mao Tse-tung thought. I was appointed to work on the reception committee. There were many practical problems to be solved. The Red Guards influenced me. We discussed a good deal. They said that everything that didn't accord with Mao Tse-tung thought must go. Act like Chairman Mao, they said. Don't be afraid.

(Jan Myrdal and Gun Kessle, *The Revolution Continued*, Penguin Books, 1970)

Source 30

A TEACHER CHANGES HIS ATTITUDE

In Wachi Middle School, one member of staff made the following statement: 'I was a graduate from the old University. I am teaching Chinese language and literature. Before the Cultural Revolution I concentrated on my professional study and I had no need of political study. At that time my aim was to become a specialist in order to make an easier living and to have a cosy family. In those days I used to tell students: "Study diligently and then you can go to the university to study further and finally you will become a specialist". I never said a word about "You should serve the people, heart and soul". I never allowed the students to criticise me. If I made a mistake I always put on an air—I was always correct.

During the Cultural Revolution . . . my students had a chat with me to change my thinking and ideology. They pointed out

Commune member Chou Shu-ching earnestly studies Chairman Mao quotations with the help of her little daughter

Young people discussing the Proletarian Cultural Revolution

Little Red Soldiers, on parade

59

"You should remould your world outlook" . . . I came to realise that it is not the sole purpose for students to study intellectual knowledge at school. If every person likes to seek personal fame and gain, who will build our country and who will make the revolution in China and in the world as well?'

(From an article by Godfrey N. Brown, in the *Times Educational Supplement,* 14 November, 1975)

Source 31

PART-WORK, PART-STUDY SCHOOL

A child's introduction to productive work takes place in the kindergarten and the primary school where a certain amount of simple agricultural and industrial work is done. By the time he or she reaches middle school, about 30 per cent of the pupil's time will be spent in working in a factory or commune or in the school workshops. During the 70 per cent of time spent in study the pupil will undertake courses in 'Foundations of Industry' embracing physics and chemistry, and 'Foundations of Agriculture' which includes biology as well as agronomy . . .

Most middle schools in the towns have a factory that has, as it were, adopted it. The school itself remains under the municipal or district education bureau, but the factory it is associated with will send a worker, or workers to determine the nature of the productive work done in the school workshops, will supply materials and know-how, will buy or sell the product, will send workers to give talks at the school and sometimes supply workers to act as classroom teachers and textbook compilers. This is all in addition to receiving pupils as production workers in the factory itself for a certain period each year.

(R. Howard, *Education and Production in China Now,* No. 56)

Children in Yenan helping to build foundations for an extension to their school

School children making a pavement in Sian

6 PROTECTING THE HOMELAND

In 1949 the Chinese believed that they faced enemies on many sides. For the first two decades after 1949 their main fears centred on Taiwan (called Formosa by many Europeans), Korea, Vietnam and the border with India.

TAIWAN

Chiang Kai-shek and his Kuomintang established themselves on Taiwan after their defeat by the Red Army. At first, even though she still recognised Chiang Kai-shek as the real ruler of China, America declared that she would not give him any aid.

When the Korean War began in 1950, however, the Americans saw that their action in support of South Korea would be threatened if the Communists occupied Taiwan. President Truman therefore ordered the American Seventh Fleet to patrol the straits between the island and the mainland.

Under American protection of this sort, Chiang built up an army of 300 000 troops. He made it

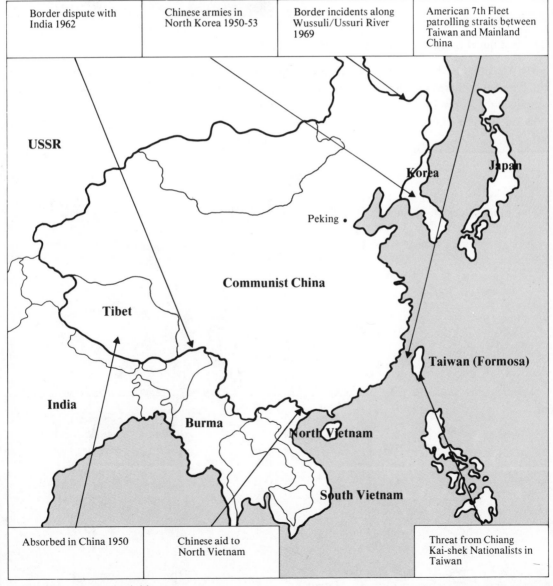

Border dispute with India 1962	Chinese armies in North Korea 1950-53	Border incidents along Wussuli/Ussuri River 1969	American 7th Fleet patrolling straits between Taiwan and Mainland China

Absorbed in China 1950	Chinese aid to North Vietnam		Threat from Chiang Kai-shek Nationalists in Taiwan

Map 8: China and her neighbours

clear that his aim was to invade mainland China to win it back for the Kuomintang, but America said that she would not support him in such an adventure. Despite two minor outbreaks of trouble in 1955 and 1958, the expected Communist attack on Taiwan did not come. With the passing of the years, as Chiang grew into an old man, no longer fit enough to lead an active campaign, the threat to Communist China from Taiwan came to seem unreal.

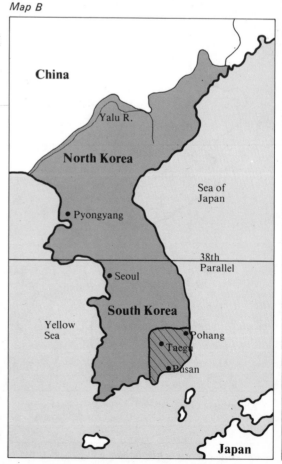

Chiang Kai-shek and his wife wave to the crowds celebrating National Day, the 'Double Tenth' anniversary, Taiwan, October 1968

KOREA

The first threat to the security of China's frontiers came in 1950 when trouble flared up in Korea.

Between 1910 and 1945 Korea had been controlled by Japan. After the Japanese surrender in 1945, the Russians occupied the North of Korea and the Americans, the South. Both powers agreed to leave as soon as the Koreans elected their own government. But it proved impossible for the different Korean political groups to agree to a united government. Four years later the country remained divided at the

Map 9: Korean War Map A

Map B

China

Yalu R.

North Korea

Sea of
Japan

• Pyongyang

38th
Parallel

• Seoul

South Korea

·Yellow
Sea

•Pohang
• Taegu
•Pusan

Japan

China

Yalu R.

North Korea

Sea of
Japan

• Pyongyang

38th
Parallel

• Seoul

South Korea

Yellow
Sea

Pohang
Taegu
•Pusan

Japan

Map C

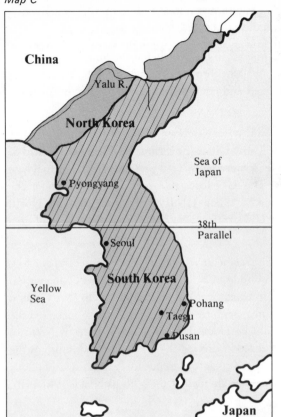

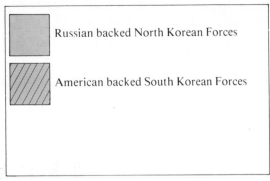

	Russian backed North Korean Forces
	American backed South Korean Forces

China

Yalu R.

North Korea

Pyongyang

Sea of Japan

38th Parallel

Seoul

Yellow Sea

South Korea

Pohang
Taegu
Pusan

Japan

Map D

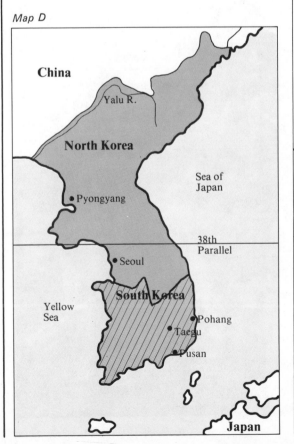

China

Yalu R.

North Korea

Pyongyang

Sea of Japan

38th Parallel

Seoul

Yellow Sea

South Korea

Pohang
Taegu
Pusan

Japan

Map E

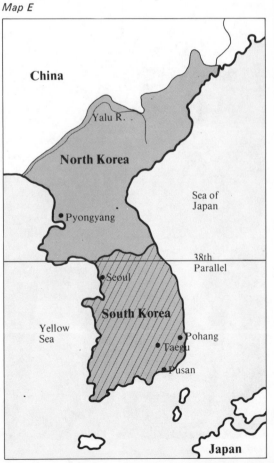

China

Yalu R.

North Korea

Pyongyang

Sea of Japan

38th Parallel

Seoul

Yellow Sea

South Korea

Pohang
Taegu
Pusan

Japan

63

38th parallel. There was a Communist government in the North and an American-backed government under Syngman Rhee in the South. In 1948-9 the Russians and the Americans withdrew their armies leaving behind a United Nations Commission to try to unite the two halves of the country.

The UN Commission had little success. The governments in the North and the South each seemed determined to try and reunite Korea by force. Raids and clashes broke out along the 38th parallel. After a dispute in June 1950, the North Korean army, trained and equipped by the Russians, invaded the South (see Map A).

The United Nations Security Council declared that this was a clear case of North Korean aggression and called upon UN members to help the South. The United States government, fearing the spread of Communism, responded immediately. American soldiers were transferred to Korea from Japan. These were joined by smaller groups from other nations. This UN force in Korea was placed under the command of the American, General MacArthur (Sources 32 and 33). By September 1950 the North Koreans had over-run almost all the South and the UN armies were forced back into a small area around Pusan (see Map B).

General MacArthur's way of dealing with this situation seemed to threaten China (Sources 34 and 35). The UN force struck back at the North Koreans and, although Chou En-lai warned that China would intervene if they crossed the 38th parallel, this is just what they did (see Map C). In fact General MacArthur not only sent his army well into North Korea, capturing Pyongyang, he also increased the tension further by suggesting that China's coast should be blockaded and Chinese industrial centres should be bombed. The Chinese army eventually succeeded in driving the UN force back south of the 38th parallel (see Map D). After bitter fighting, an armistice was agreed in July 1953. But no satisfactory solution was reached at the Peace Talks and Korea remained divided at the 38th parallel (see Map E).

Red Army soldiers

BIOGRAPHY: CHOU EN-LAI (1898-1976)

Early years

Chou En-lai was born in Kiangsu province in 1898 and was educated in mission schools. He first came into contact with Communist ideas in 1917 when studying in Japan. In 1920 he went to France to continue his studies and by 1922 he became the organiser for the Chinese Communist Party in Europe. On his return to China in 1924, Chou became deputy political director of Chiang Kai-shek's Whampoa Military Academy.

During the years of civil war against the Kuomintang, Chou became an important member of the Chinese Communist Party. When Mao and the Red Army were driven from the Kiangsi soviet in 1934 by Chiang Kai-shek, Chou went with them on the Long March. During the March, Chou was elected vice-chairman of the party under Mao and from this time on Chou became Mao's faithful supporter. Afterwards he became the CCP's chief negotiator with the Nationalists during the war against Japan.

His work for the People's Republic of China

When the People's Republic was founded in 1949, Chou became Prime Minister and Foreign Minister. Although he gave up his position as Foreign Minister in 1958 he remained largely responsible for Chinese foreign affairs until his death.

Chou believed that China should play an important part in world affairs and he soon established himself as an international diplomat and a brilliant negotiator. He represented China at the Geneva Conference on Indo-China/Vietnam in 1954. In 1957 he visited Poland and Hungary and established contacts with Communist countries in eastern Europe.

During the 1960s Chou also developed friendships with countries in Africa and the Middle East. After China's relations with Russia became strained in the 1960s, Chou favoured a policy of friendship with the USA. In 1971/2, Dr Kissinger and President Nixon visited Peking for talks with Mao and Chou En-lai.

Within China, Chou was a Prime Minister with moderate political views. During the Cultural Revolution he tried hard to hold back extremists and criticised the Red Guards for their sieges of foreign embassies.

At the peak of his domestic and international power Chou's health began to fail. When he died in January 1976, Chou was deeply mourned by millions of Chinese and by Mao Tse-tung, his old comrade and friend.

Source 32

AMERICA RESPONDS TO THE SECURITY COUNCIL CALL

Washington, June 27

President Truman issued the following statement shortly after noon today:
In Korea the Government forces, which were armed to prevent border raids and to preserve internal security, were attacked

by invading forces from North Korea. The Security Council of the United Nations called upon the invading troops to cease hostilities and to withdraw to the 38th parallel. This they have not done but, on the contrary, have pressed the attack. The Security Council called upon all members of the United Nations to render every assistance to the United Nations in the execution of this resolution. In these circumstances I have ordered United States air and sea forces to give the Korean Government troops cover and support.

(*The Times,* June 28, 1950)

Source 33

THE CHINESE VIEW OF THE INVASION OF SOUTH KOREA

The attack of the puppet government of Syngman Rhee on the Korean People's Democratic Republic, made at the bidding of the U.S. Government, was a premeditated move of the U.S.A. designed to create a pretext for U.S. invasion of Formosa, Korea, Vietnam, and the Philippines . . . No matter what obstructive action the American imperialists may take, Formosa is part of China, and will remain so for ever . . . The people of our country will fight as one man for the liberation of Formosa from the grasp of the American aggressors.

(*Statement by Chou En-lai,* quoted in Keesing's Contemporary Archives, July 1–8, 1950)

General MacArthur

Source 34

CHINA FEARS AMERICAN AGGRESSION

The Chinese people are fully entitled to charge the U.S.A. with provocation and aggression against China. Many Chinese citizens, righteously indignant, are expressing a desire to help the Korean people to resist American aggression. Facts have shown that the aim of U.S. aggression in Korea is not only Korea itself but also the extension of aggression to China. The Chinese government repeats its demand for a peaceful settlement of the Korean issue by the immediate withdrawal of all foreign troops. The Chinese people ardently love peace but will not be afraid to take action against aggressors and no aggression will intimidate it.

(*Chinese Note* delivered to the U.N. on 15 November 1950 quoted in *KCA,* December 2–9, 1950)

Source 35

THE AMERICAN VIEW OF CHINA'S REACTION TO THE U.N. ADVANCE

New York, November 28.

General MacArthur . . . described the situation in a special United Nations communiqué.

'Enemy reactions developed in the course of our assault operations of the past four days disclose that a major regiment of the Chinese continental armed forces in an army, corps, and divisional organization of an aggregate strength of over 200,000 men is now arrayed against the United Nations force in North Korea . . . Consequently we face an entirely new war.'

(*The Times,* 29 November, 1950)

VIETNAM

Before 1949 Vietnam had been a French colony. At the end of the Second World War, France was unwilling to surrender her power, but the Vietnamese nationalists (Vietminh) wanted their independence. Under their Communist leader, Ho Chi-minh, they defeated the French. At the Peace Conference in 1954 it was agreed that the French should leave and that the Vietminh should withdraw their forces north of the 17th parallel. The Communists set up a government of their own in Hanoi, in opposition to the Vietnamese government in Saigon.

Fighting broke out between North and South in 1959 and from the beginning the United States supported the South. When the Americans began to send in troops, the Chinese could not ignore the threat to their borders, but China sent only supplies like food and arms to the Vietcong (Communists). It seems they did not want to become directly involved in another war with the United States. After the Vietnam war ended in 1973, China continued her friendship towards the Vietcong with a promise of military and economic aid (Source 36).

Source 36

FRIENDSHIP BETWEEN VIETNAM AND COMMUNIST CHINA CONTINUES AFTER THE WAR IS OVER

We are bringing with us the feelings of warm friendship and deep gratitude of the Vietnamese people, the Viet Nam Workers' Party and the Government of the Democratic Republic of Viet Nam towards Chairman Mao Tse-tung, the great leader of the Chinese people and the beloved and respected friend of the Vietnamese people, and towards the Chinese Communist Party, the Government and the fraternal people of China, who have unswervingly and wholeheartedly supported and assisted the Vietnamese people's patriotic struggle against U.S. aggression and for social construction.

> (Comrade Le Duan of North Viet Nam, addressing a meeting in Peking, June 7, 1973, quoted in *Viet Nam* (periodical) 182 of 1973)

Map 10: Vietnam, 1946–54

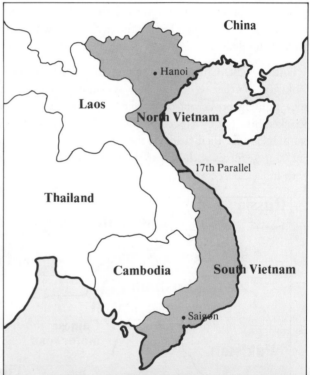

A Chinese government delegation visits a unit of the Vietnam People's Army Airforce, March 1971

BORDER WITH INDIA

Another region in which the Chinese felt insecure was the southern Himalayan border. Historically, Tibet was always considered part of China, but when the British had ruled in India they had been the most influential power in that region. British rule in India had come to an end in 1947 so, when the Communists came to power in China in 1949, they felt that their position was strong enough to assert their authority over Tibet. In 1950 they sent a force into Tibet, claiming that it was 'an integral part of China', and although the Indian government protested, there was nothing they could do in practice to alter the situation.

The Tibetan ruler, the Dalai Lama, was allowed to remain in charge in Tibet under Chinese protection, but there were clashes between the traditional Buddhist way of life and the new Communist plans. In 1959 a tribal dispute grew into a wider rebellion and thousands of refugees, including the Dalai Lama, fled into India. China dealt firmly with the rebellion, while the Indian government tried not to appear hostile to China, although they felt sympathetic towards the Dalai Lama and the Tibetans.

In bringing Tibet under her control, China brought the Red Army to the borders of India. Precisely where this border was had never been agreed. When the British ruled in India they had drawn what was called the McMahon Line in the east, and now the Chinese were claiming some land which lay on the Indian side of this.

Further west, China was planning to build a new road through Askai Chin to link Tibet with Sinkiang. In order to do this she was claiming land which not everyone agreed was hers. In October 1962 fighting broke out in Ladakh, the north-eastern corner of Kashmir. It is not clear which side attacked first, but by November the Indian troops had been forced back. The Chinese had secured just enough land for their road. At the same time there had been fighting at the eastern end of the border, but Chinese forces withdrew to the McMahon Line. It seemed that Mao did not want an extended war with India (Source 37).

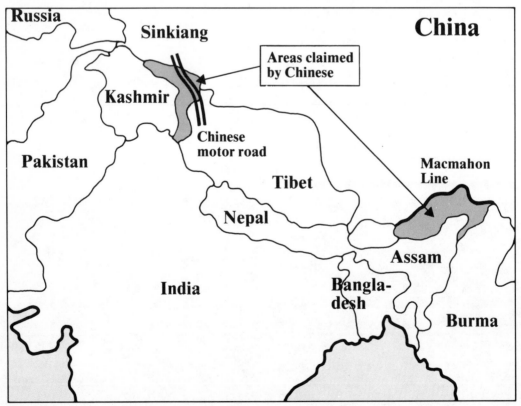

Map 11: China's border with India

The Dalai Lama (6th from left) with his Khamba warrior guard during his flight to India, 1959

7 CHINA AND RUSSIA

EARLY FRIENDSHIP

Soon after the Communists came to power in 1949, Mao paid a visit to Moscow. He was looking to the Soviet Union for continued support—partly against any foreign attempt to restore Chiang Kai-shek, and partly in the task of rebuilding China's war-damaged industry and agriculture. A treaty of friendship was signed on 14 February 1950 and was warmly welcomed by spokesmen of both countries (Source 38).

Poster proclaiming the friendship between the Chinese and Russian peoples

*Krushchev and Mao in Peking as
differences began to reach breaking point*

For the next few years the alliance brought considerable benefit to China. Russian political support helped China through the difficult years of the Korean War and her economic aid played an essential part in the success of the first Five-Year Plan. At the same time China seemed to have some influence on Russia. When there was a rebellion in Poland in the autumn of 1956, China argued strongly against Russian intervention because there was no question that Poland would cease to be a Communist country. But a few weeks later, when Krushchev sent Russian tanks and troops into Hungary, China came out strongly in his support, because she believed that this rebellion would have undone the work of the Communist revolution.

Source 38

TWO STATEMENTS MADE FOLLOWING THE SIGNING OF THE TREATY BETWEEN CHINA AND THE SOVIET UNION

The Treaty of Friendship . . . based on respect for the principle of equality, state independence and national sovereignty, seals the historic bonds between the peoples of the Soviet Union and China.

(*Vyshinsky*, Soviet Foreign Minister)

People can see that the unity of the two peoples of China and the Soviet Union, already solidified through a treaty, will be everlasting, unbreakable and inseparable by any people. This kind of unity not only will affect the prosperity of China and the Soviet Union but will certainly affect the future of humanity and the victory of world peace and justice.

(*Mao Tse-tung*, 14th and 17th February, 1950)

THE RELATIONSHIP BECOMES STRAINED

The Chinese now say that the unity between their country and Russia in the mid-1950s was only temporary. Certainly strains began to appear soon afterwards. In November 1957, on the fortieth anniversary of the Russian Revolution, an important meeting of Communist and Workers' Parties was held in Moscow. The purpose of the meeting was to present a united Communist front to the western world, and to the United States in particular.

Krushchev, the Russian leader, had argued that with the development of nuclear weapons, 'There are only two ways: either peaceful co-existence [between Communist and non-Communist countries] or the most destructive war in history' (Source 39).

The Chinese thought the Russians were giving up the struggle to spread the influence of Communism. Mao said that he, too, wanted to strive for peace, but the threat of war must not be allowed to halt the progress of the revolution. The Chinese leaders believed the Russian leaders were retreating from the pure teaching of Marx and Lenin and were betraying the Communist cause throughout the world (Source 40).

Source 39

KRUSHCHEV DECLARES THAT COMMUNISM AND CAPITALISM CAN EXIST TOGETHER PEACEFULLY

The questions concerned were the peaceful co-existence of the two systems, the possibility of averting wars in the present epoch and the forms of transition to socialism in various countries.

We believe the countries with differing social systems can do more than exist side by side. It is necessary to proceed further, to improve relations, strengthen confidence between countries and co-operate.

There is no other way out in current conditions. In fact, there are only two paths: either peaceful co-existence or the most devastating war in history. There is no third way.

(*Krushchev's Speech*, February, 1956)

Source 40

CHINA ATTACKS KRUSHCHEV'S POLICY OF PEACEFUL CO-EXISTENCE

For several years there have been differences within the international communist movement . . . The central issue is . . . whether or not to accept the fact that the people still living under the imperialist and capitalist system . . . need to make revolution and whether or not to accept the fact that the people already on the Socialist road . . . need to carry their revolution forward to the end.

5. The following erroneous views should be repudiated . . . that the contradiction between the proletariat and the bourgeoisie can be resolved without a proletarian revolution in each country and that the contradiction between the oppressed nations and imperialism can be resolved without revolution . . .

(*Letter from the Chinese Government to the Soviet Government,* 14 June 1963, quoted in *KCA*, August 10–17, 1963)

BITTER DISAGREEMENTS

During the next five years disagreements between the two countries grew more bitter. In 1960 Russia withdrew her technicians and aid from China, and China crticised Russia openly, particularly over the

Chinese frontier guards on the alert

Cuba missile crisis in 1962. Each country accused the other of provoking incidents along the border that separated them. The disputed territory had been forcibly ceded to Russia in 1858 and 1860, when China was too weak to resist. Tension grew as each side built up its forces in the area.

The clash that had been threatening for so long broke out in 1969. Between March and August, in a series of incidents, shots were exchanged between the border guards, causing casualties on both sides. Each accused the other of being the aggressor and for a time there seemed to be a danger of full-scale war (Sources 41 and 42).

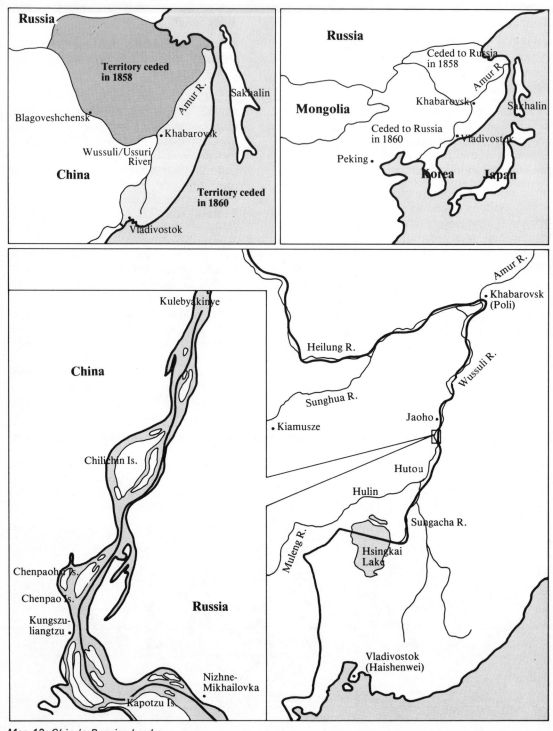

Map 12: China's Russian border

Source 41

CHINESE ACCOUNT OF THE INCIDENT ON AUGUST 13, 1969

. . . the Soviet side sent two helicopters, dozens of tanks and armoured vehicles, and several hundred armed troops to intrude into the Tiehliehkti area . . . who penetrated a depth of two kilometres, unwarrantedly fired at the Chinese frontier guards on normal patrol duty, killing and wounding many of them on the spot, and closed in on them. Driven beyond the limits of forbearance, the Chinese frontier guards were compelled to fight back in self-defence.

(*KCA,* November 1–8, 1969)

Source 42

SOVIET UNION ACCOUNT OF THE INCIDENT ON AUGUST 13, 1969

The armed provocation staged by the Chinese authorities on the Soviet Chinese border was planned in advance. On the previous day, August 12, Soviet frontier guards observed that Army units were being moved up on the Chinese side of this section of the frontier, that there were intensive troop movements, and that communication lines were being put up. To avert a worsening of the situation the Soviet frontier authorities called on the frontier guards of the People's Republic of China to send a representative for talks. The latter declined . . .

(*KCA,* November 1–8, 1969)

Soviet tanks moving into disputed territory to the west of China's Chenpao island

Soviet troops intrude into the Chenpao island area. Chinese frontier guards warn them not to intrude further

A Soviet tank heads for the east bank Wussuli River pursued by of the Chinese frontier guards

Although the fighting died down, no progress was made towards a peaceful solution of the problem. The differences between the two were kept alive as the war of words continued to issue increasingly from Peking and Moscow.

The Chinese believe the Russian leaders are afraid of what is happening in China. It is easy for Russians to criticise what they know and see of life in western countries, but if they were allowed to know what is happening in China, this would inspire them to demand further revolutionary changes in Russia, and this, say the Chinese, is the last thing the Russian leaders want.

8 CHINA AND THE REST OF THE WORLD

Since the late 1960s China's position in the world has changed in some significant ways. She has built more links with Europe and America through diplomatic exchanges, trade relations and increasing cultural contacts.

民族联合起来！

74 | *Nixon and Chou review the Chinese guard at Peking Airport*

THE UNITED NATIONS

One of the most obvious ways of recognising China's importance was to admit her to the United Nations. From 1950 onwards the proposal to admit China to the General Assembly had been debated on numerous occasions, but American influence had ensured that it was defeated. The permanent seat on the Security Council reserved for China was occupied by a representative from Chiang Kai-shek's Nationalist government in Taiwan (Source 43).

In October 1971, however, a large enough vote was cast in favour of Communist China. She took her seat in the General Assembly and at the same time she replaced the Nationalist representative on the Security Council.

Deputy Foreign Minister Chiao Kuan-hua and permanent UN representative Huang Hua at the UN, November 1971

Source 43

U.N. VOTES ON THE ADMISSION OF THE PEOPLE'S REPUBLIC OF CHINA

Year	For China	Against	Abstention
1950	16	32	10
1955	12	42	6
1960	34	42	22
1965	47	47	20
1970	51	48	25
1971	76	35	17

NUCLEAR POWER

Some people believe that the one thing which made other countries take China seriously was that she developed her own atomic bomb. The first time she exploded such a bomb successfully was in October 1964. She was only the fifth country to do so.

Previously Mao had described the atomic bomb as a 'paper tiger', asserting that China, with her huge population, could survive a nuclear war better than any other nation. But in 1963 the US, Russia and Britain had signed the nuclear test ban treaty, outlawing atmospheric tests. Mao saw this as a way for the big powers to control nuclear weapons and he felt the Chinese could no longer rely on the Soviet nuclear deterrent to protect them from the US. Later Russia herself seemed a threat.

Testing continued and China exploded her first hydrogen bomb in 1967. Her scientists demonstrated the progress that they had made when China launched her first satellite in April 1970.

Without doubt China must be regarded as having reached the front rank in technology, both for its peaceful as well as its military uses (Source 44).

Stamp commemorating the launching of China's first satellite

China's first hydrogen bomb explosion

Source 44

CHINA'S EXPLANATION OF HER NUCLEAR POLICY

The successful explosion of China's first hydrogen bomb on June 17, 1967, represents another leap in the development of China's nuclear weapons. It marks the entry of the development of China's nuclear weapons into an entirely new stage. This is another great victory of Mao Tse-tung's thought! A fresh splendid achievement of the great proletarian cultural revolution!

Man is the factor that decides victory or defeat in war. The conducting of neces-sary and limited nuclear tests and the development of nuclear weapons by China are entirely for the purpose of defence, with the ultimate aim of abolishing nuclear weapons. At no time and in no circumstances will China be the first to use nuclear weapons. As in the past, the Chinese people and government will continue to make common efforts and carry on an unswerving struggle together with all the other peace-loving people and countries of the world for the noble aim of completely prohibiting and thoroughly destroying nuclear weapons.

(from an article in *China Pictorial*, 1967, a magazine produced in Peking)

THE THIRD WORLD

It is not only by becoming a nuclear power that China has increased her influence in the rest of the world. As early as the winter of 1963–64, Chou En-lai had toured Africa and the Middle East in an effort to win the friendship of developing countries and to offer them economic aid.

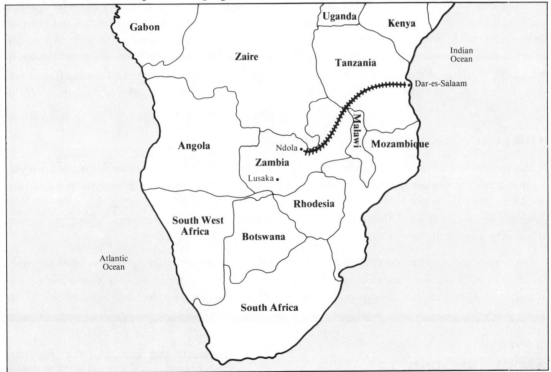

Map 13: The Tan-Zam Railway

One big project in which China was involved was the building of the Tan-Zam Railway. Tanzania and Zambia had wanted to build such a railway for a long time. They needed it to carry the copper from the rich mines of Zambia to the coast, for export to the rest of the world, without having to go through South Africa. They lacked the money and the skill, however, to build it themselves.

The work became possible only when China offered to help with a large loan of money and advice from her skilled engineers. Three years were spent in planning and clearing the route through difficult jungle and mountain country, and in 1975 the railway was completed, two years ahead of schedule (Source 45).

President Kaunda unveiling a plaque after the official opening of the Tan-Zam railway

China regards the provision of economic aid as an important way of spreading her influence and of showing that Communism can bring peace and prosperity to a country (Source 46). Her declared purpose is to develop a group of countries which will be independent in world politics and not take orders from either America or Russia. However, China maintains that she has no wish to lead this group and so become a Super-Power herself. Indeed, China has repeatedly emphasised the dangers of seeing the world as divided into two camps, either grouped around the Super-Powers, Russia and America; or the rich nations on the one hand and the poorer countries, known as the Third World, on the other (Source 47).

THE EUROPEAN ECONOMIC COMMUNITY

China was the first Communist country, apart from Yugoslavia, to send an ambassador to the European Community. She obviously hopes that a strong united Europe will be another respected power in the world, to offset the Super-Powers. Another possible reason for her support, which China herself does not mention, is that it would be in her interests if Russia became more concerned about her western frontiers and less concerned with keeping troops on her borders with China.

Friendly relations are in the European Community's interests too. It recognises the need for more trade links with the east, and China possesses an estimated 25–30 per cent of the world's main minerals. So there are good reasons on both sides for the increasing cooperation.

Source 45

AFRICAN RESPONSE TO CHINESE AID

. . . We are extremely grateful to the Chinese People's Republic for their help in the railway project; we are grateful for the spirit in which the offer of assistance was made, and for the manner in which this assistance is being given . . .

Let me state quite clearly that we

appreciate this loan, and we appreciate the fact that it is interest-free. We greatly appreciate all this help with the building of our railway. And — I repeat — the Chinese people have not asked us to become Communists in order to qualify for this loan! They know that we would not sell our independence, even for the railway; and they have never at any point suggested that we should change any of our policies — internal or external —

because of their help with this railway.

(Julius K. Nyerere, *Freedom and Development*, Oxford University Press, 1973)

Source 46

CHINESE ECONOMIC AID

. . . With the worsening plight of the underdeveloped countries very much in the news, no assessment of China would be complete without a review of its role in promoting development in the Third World.

'Promoting development', rather than simply providing aid, is a more accurate description of China's position than of any other country's. For China is itself part of the Third World, grappling with its most typical problems on its own soil and gradually transforming the very conditions that have given rise to world confrontation between rich and poor . . .

In China's view a country cannot develop in the true sense except by its own efforts. A strategy based on self-reliance accepts development aid from outside as a subsidiary prop to the economy, but never as its main support . . .

A condition of Chinese aid is that both specialists and other workers who do a tour of duty in a foreign country are paid according to the standards in force in that country. As the standard of living in most developing countries is low, this reduces costs considerably. Fully half the expense of aid is normally due to wages and salaries, under which head the Chinese would take less than half as much as others. In the case of medical services it has been calculated that the overall cost of a scheme may be reduced to about a quarter when it is being provided by the Chinese.

(from an article by P. A. Timberlake in *The Times*, 30 September, 1975)

President Nyerere of Tanzania with Chou En-lai in Peking

Source 47

CHINA'S VIEW OF THREE WORLDS

Judging from the changes in international relations, the world today actually consists of three parts, or three worlds, that are both interconnected and in contradiction to one another. The United States and the Soviet Union make up the First World. The developing countries in Asia, Africa, Latin America and other regions make up the Third World. The developed countries between the two make up the Second World . . .

China is a Socialist country, and a developing country as well. China belongs to the Third World . . . China is not a Super-Power, nor will she ever seek to be one. What is a Super-Power? A Super-Power is an imperialist country which everywhere subjects other countries to its aggression, interference, control, subversion or plunder and strives for world hegemony . . . If one day China should change her colour and turn into a Super-Power, if she too should play the tyrant in the world . . . the people of the world should identify her social-imperialism, expose it, oppose it and work together with the Chinese people to overthrow it.

(from Teng Hsiao-ping's speech to the United Nations General Assembly 10 April 1975 printed in *Peking Review,* Vol. 17, No. 16, 19 April, 1975)

CHINA:SUPER POWER?
CHINA AND THE OTHER GREAT POWERS: SOME STATISTICS

Population in millions mid 1973 estimates

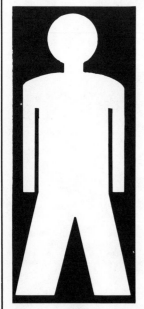

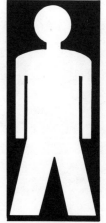

China	USA	USSR	Britain	France	Japan	India
780	213	252	55	52	108	584

Land Areas Million km²

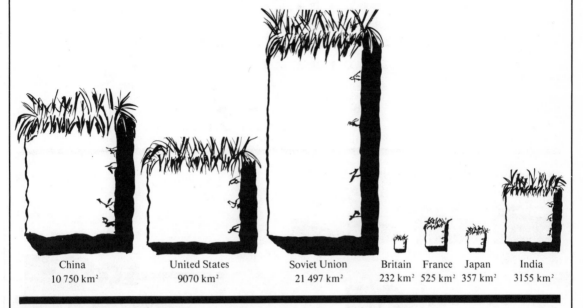

China
10 750 km²

United States
9070 km²

Soviet Union
21 497 km²

Britain
232 km²

France
525 km²

Japan
357 km²

India
3155 km²

Wealth The total wealth of a country is usually called its
Gross National Product (GNP) US $ billion (1969)

China 58

United States 732

USSR 245

Britain 89

France 105

Japan 124

India 49

Total Armed Forces Thousands (1970)

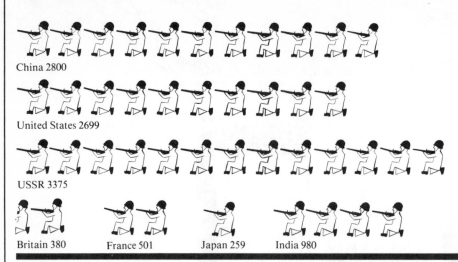

China 2800

United States 2699

USSR 3375

Britain 380   France 501   Japan 259   India 980

Expenditure on Armed Forces US $ Millions

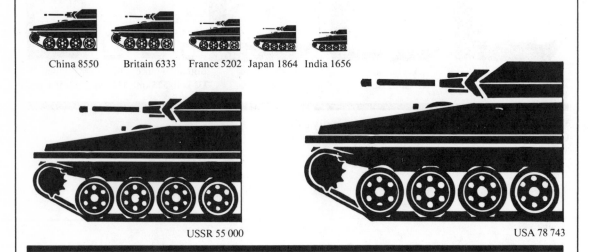

China 8550   Britain 6333   France 5202   Japan 1864   India 1656

USSR 55 000

USA 78 743

Aid to Other Countries Millions of pounds sterling

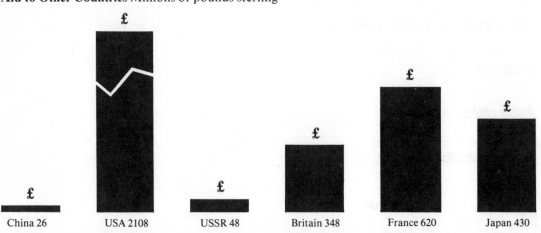

China 26   USA 2108   USSR 48   Britain 348   France 620   Japan 430

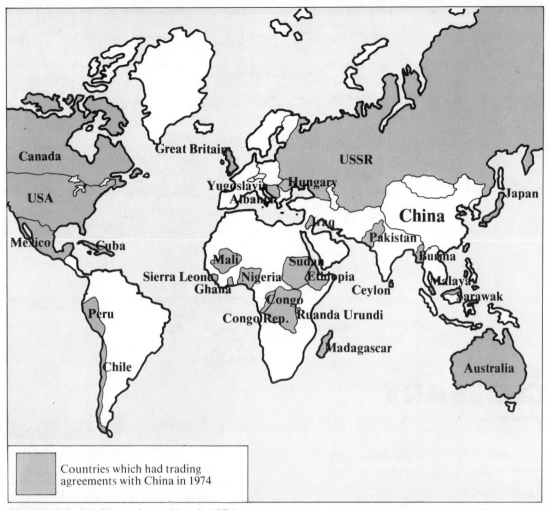

Countries which had trading
agreements with China in 1974

Map 14: China's influence in world trade, 1974

*The President of the Community receiving His Excellency Mr Li Lien-pi,
Ambassador of the Chinese Peoples Republic*

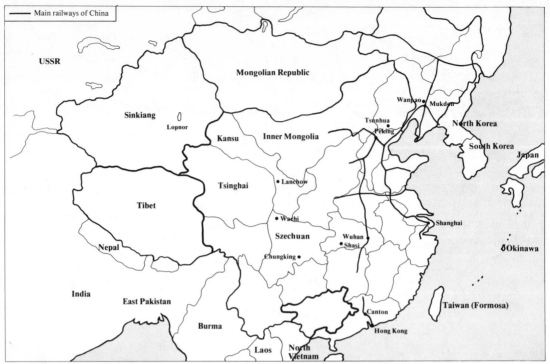

Map 15: Communist China, 1970

GLOSSARY

agitation—debate, discussion, stirring up the people

aggressors—those who attack others without cause or provocation

averting—avoiding

Bolsheviks—members of the Bolshevik Party. This party was established in 1904 when a majority (*bolshinto*) of the Russian Social Democratic Party decided to adopt Lenin's proposal to restrict membership of the party to a body of professional revolutionaries dedicated to overthrowing the Russian Empire and establishing a Communist State. They came to power in Russia in the November 1917 Revolution.

bourgeoisie—the middle class, including small businessmen, professional men such as lawyers, teachers and doctors, small farmers, master craftsmen

bureaucracy—the civil service, government officials

cadres—dedicated party members who make up teams which go out into the countryside and organize the peasants into village associations; they explain Party policy and assist the peasants in carrying it out

capitalists—people who own property such as a business or land; they make a profit from it for themselves out of the work done by workers and peasants on their behalf for a fixed wage

capitalist society—a system in which a relatively small number of private individuals own all the industries and land, from which they take all the profit. The rest of the population have to earn their living by working for them in return for fixed wages. A capitalist society is thus divided into different classes (upper, middle, lower) on the basis of the distribution of property and wealth.

CCP—the abbreviation for the *Chinese Communist Party*

centralised—governed or controlled from the centre

coexistence—living together, side by side

commune—an almost self-sufficient community made up of a number of co-operative farms and local factories, banks and schools. Each commune contains about 25 000 people, divided into brigades, and sub-divided into teams; they are sent to work wherever their labour is necessary to the commune

concessions—areas of China taken over in the second half of the nineteenth century by the Western powers (chiefly Britain, France,

84

Germany and Russia) where their citizens could live and carry on their trades and businesses, protected from Chinese competition. These areas came under the laws of the foreign country concerned, and had their own police and courts. They were increasingly resented by Chinese nationalists.

consequences—results

consigning—handing over

consulate—belonging to the office of the consul, the official representative of his government in a foreign city

corps—body of troops for a special purpose

corruption—bribery, buying favours for personal profit or advantage

culminated—built up to a climax

cuspidors—spittoons

despots—tyrannical rulers

deteriorate—get worse, degenerate

discredit—question the truth, bring into disrepute

dividends—sums of money from the profits of a company payable to the shareholders (people who own part of the company)

domestic oppressors—people who rule their fellow countrymen harshly and exploit them

duress—pressure, threat of imprisonment or force

dynasty—line of hereditary rulers

egalitarian—believing in the equality of all people, providing equal opportunity for all the people

epoch—era, period in history

evident—obvious

facilitate—make easy

faction—political party or group

factionalism—each political group looking after its own interests, quarrelling with its rivals for power

factor—agent, means of contributing to a result

fervour—enthusiasm

formulated—made up, laid down

Fourth Front Army—a section of the Red Army, commanded by Chang Kuo t'ao in 1935, and containing about 50 000 men

gratification—satisfaction

guerrilla bands—small groups of soldiers who avoid taking on the enemy in open battle where

possible; guerrillas prefer such tactics as the ambush where they can use their numbers to best advantage. They travel light, move fast and live off the land, relying on the help and protection of the local population

hegemony—leadership

HQ—the abbreviation for Headquarters

humanity—mankind, the human race

humiliation—indignity, shame

ideology—the ideas and beliefs at the basis of a political theory or system, such as Communism or Fascism

Imperialists—the government and people of a powerful, developed country who take or try to take economic and/or political control of a weaker and less developed country

insolence—contempt, insulting manner

insurrection—rebellion, uprising

institutions—established laws and ways of conducting affairs in government, business, education etc.

integral—inseparable from the whole

intellectuals—well educated people who have a wide knowledge of one or more subjects, have developed good reasoning powers, and who are interested in ideas

jujubes—berry-like fruit with a stone at the centre

KMT—the abbreviation for the Kuomintang

Kuomintang—the Chinese Nationalist Party created by Sung Chiao-jen who united various republican groups in 1912. It was originally modelled on the ancient Chinese secret societies and its general aims were the establishment of national unity and parliamentary democracy. Sun Yat-sen revived the party in 1922–3 with the help of Russian advisers. The Kuomintang was modelled on the Russian Bolshevik Party. Although it was not Communist, it cooperated with the Communists at first. Its aims were based on Sun Yat-sen's three principles—national democracy, political democracy and economic democracy.

Chiang Kai-shek took over the leadership of the party on the death of Sun Yat-sen in 1927. Chiang broke with the CCP; apart from a truce during the war against Japan, the two parties remained rivals for the control of China until 1949, when the remnants of the KMT fled with Chiang to Taiwan (Formosa).

legacy—something handed down to others when a person dies

legations—the official residences of foreign diplomats and representatives

li—a Chinese measurement of distance, about half a kilometre

liberation—freedom, release from oppression, usually by the establishment of a new regime or government

lustre—shine or gloss

Mandarin—official in the Chinese Empire

Manifesto—public declaration of policy, ideas

millet—edible seeds from a grass like plant

mobility—being able to move from one place to another easily

motive—driving, moving

munitions—armaments, ammunition and other military equipment

nationalist—following a patriotic policy of national independence for China, and freedom from foreign influence and exploitation. When spelt with a capital N, it means a member of the KMT

perpetrated—performed, committed

plausible—reasonable, believable

pledging—promising

Politburo—the ruling body of the Chinese Communist Party, consisting of eighteen members and seven alternate members who act as deputies

priority—item of first importance, the first thing to be considered

progressively—gradually

proletariat—working class

promote—advance, look after

radical—desiring fundamental reforms in the political or economic system

render—give

Republican—supporting a republican system of government, i.e. a government without a king or queen at the head, which is democratically elected

repudiated—disowned, denied

reverence—respectful treatment of somebody, as if he or she were sacred

rightist provocations—actions by people with right wing political beliefs which aim to undermine the Communist and socialist system

sampans—small Chinese boats

scruple—conscience

security—money from another source to be paid to the lender if the borrower does not repay to the loan, a safeguard

socialism—a political and economic system in which the State, on behalf of the people, owns all the industries and land, and uses its wealth to provide full employment, fair wages, good health and educational facilities, housing and welfare of all. In this system there are no capitalists

sovereignty—the legal right to absolute power

soviet—a group (or cell) of Communists which is organised democratically. The Chinese followed the Russian Boshevik example of organising revolutionary councils elected by the workers, soldiers or peasants in a particular district, to build up a network of Communist groups throughout the country to lead the masses

subjugation—brought under control by force

subversion—plotting to undermine the government

technology—scientific principles and knowledge applied to the development of new industrial processes and machinery

thesis—argument, proposition

Third World—the developing countries, in Africa or South America

traditions—age old beliefs and customs

transactions—deals

ultimatum—a final demand to take a particular action or face unpleasant consequences

unwarrantedly—without good cause

versatile—useful for many different purposes and adaptable to a variety of conditions

vice-consul—deputy for the Consul, the official representative of his government in a foreign city. The consul looks after the interests of people from his own country who live or visit there

warlords—military governors of provinces in the Empire, who were in charge of the troops of the Chinese army stationed in their province. Some recruited and trained their own militia too, and used the soldiers under their command as a private army to increase their own power. At times large parts of China were effectively controlled by rival warlords

ACKNOWLEDGEMENTS

The authors and publishers are grateful to the following for permission to reproduce copyright material:

Photographs

page 4 *bronze leopards* and *white pottery jug*, Robert Harding Associates, © Times Newspapers Ltd; *Great Wall*, Mansell Collection;

page 6 *peasant family*, Popperfoto;

page 7 *English officers*, Radio Times Hulton Picture Library;

page 8 *a Mandarin and family*, Church Missionary Society, London;

page 9 *Empress Tzu-hsi*, Mansell Collection;

page 10 *Emperor Pu-yi*, Mansell Collection;

page 11 *cutting pigtails*, Church Missionary Society, London;

page 12 *Yuan Shi-kai*, Popperfoto; *Li Yuan-hung*, Popperfoto; *Chang Tso-lin*, Radio Times Hulton Picture Library;

page 13 *May 4 demonstration*, China Pictorial, Oct. 1971;

page 14 *Mao, 1919*, Camera Press;

page 15 *Young Mao and others*, Keystone Press Agency; *Chinese children*, Barnaby's Picture Library;

page 16 *funeral of Sun Yat-sen*, Popperfoto;

page 17 *Chiang Kai-shek*, Radio Times Hulton Picture Library;

page 18 *Communists executed in Canton*, Radio Times Hulton Picture Library;

page 19 *Communists in Canton*, Radio Times Hulton Picture Library;

page 20 *peasant defence corps*, China Pictorial, Oct. 1971;

page 21 *Mao Tse-tung*, Radio Times Hulton Picture Library;

page 23 *building at Tsunyi*, Barnaby's Picture Library; *mountains near Tsunyi*, China Pictorial, Oct. 1971; *Chingkang Mountains*, China Reconstructs, 1969;

page 24 *Lolos tribesmen*, from *In Forbidden China*, Vicomte d' Ollone, T. Fisher Unwin, 1912;

page 25 *Luting Bridge*, Society for Anglo-Chinese Understanding;

page 26 *Great Snow Mountain*, China Pictorial, July 1956;

page 27 *Mekong River*, Paul Popper;

page 28 *Chinghai grasslands*, China Pictorial, July 1956; *Yenan*, Society for Anglo-Chinese Understanding; *Mao with peasants*, Marc Riboud for the John Hillelson Agency;

page 29 *Mao in cave dwelling*, Society for Anglo-Chinese Understanding;

page 30 *Mao with Chou En-lai*, Keystone Press Agency;

page 32 *Chang Hsueh-liang*, Radio Times Hulton Picture Library;

page 34 *Red Army guerrillas*, Society for Anglo-Chinese Understanding;

page 35 *Communist army on the Great Wall*, Camera Press; *peasants and soldiers*, Foreign Languages Press, Peking;

page 36 *people of Chung King*, Camera Press;

page 37 *peasant life*, Mansell Collection;

page 38 *famine victims*, Popperfoto;

page 40 *peasants and Red Army*, Foreign Languages Press, Peking;

page 41 *Chairman Mao*, Marc Riboud for the John Hillelson Agency; *Red Army soldiers* and *Red Army victory parade*, Popperfoto;

page 42 *peasant refugees* and *remains of factory*, Radio Times Hulton Picture Library;

page 43 *starving refugee*, Popperfoto;

page 44 *trial of landlord*, Popperfoto;

page 47 *peasants in Tachai*, Camera Press;

page 48 *Hsipu Brigade*, Society for Anglo-Chinese Understanding; *industry*, China Pictorial, January 1963; *girls working*, Camera Press;

page 49 *girl driving a tractor*, Popperfoto; *girls on a commune*, Camera Press; *Tachai transformed*, Central Press Photos;

page 50 *large-scale industry*, Keystone Press Agency; *peasants help to build a steel mill*, Marc Riboud for the John Hillelson Agency;

page 51 *oil refinery*, China Now, Nov. 1973;

page 52 *Nanyutai Lane*, Foreign Languages Press;

page 53 *tableau*, Camera Press;

page 54 *A People's Court*, Popperfoto; *Russian tanks*, Keystone Press Agency;

page 55 *Mao the father figure*, Camera Press;

page 56 *factory workers*, Camera Press;

page 57 *Mao*, Camera Press; *veteran soldier*, Society for Anglo-Chinese Understanding; *Red Guard posters*, and *Red Guards with Mao picture*, Central Press Photos;

page 58 *Red Guards* and *May 7 cadre school*,

Society for Anglo-Chinese Understanding; *commune members*, Foreign Languages Press; page 59 *elderly peasant*, Foreign Languages Press; *school children* and *Little Red Soldiers*, Camera Press; page 60 *children in Yenan*, China Now, Nov. 1975; *school children in Sian*, Henri Cartier-Bresson for the John Hillelson Agency; page 62 *Chiang Kai-shek and his wife*, Keystone Press Agency; page 64 *Red Army soldiers*, Popperfoto; page 65 *Chou En-lai*, Camera Press; page 66 *General MacArthur*, Popperfoto; page 67 *Chinese delegation*, Society for Anglo-Chinese Understanding; page 69 *The Dalai Lama* and *poster of friendship*, Popperfoto; page 70 *Kruschev and Mao*, Popperfoto; page 71 *Chinese frontier guards*, Society for Anglo-Chinese Understanding; page 73 *Soviet troops* (x3) Society for Anglo-Chinese Understanding; page 74 *Nixon and Chou*, Keystone Press Agency; page 75 *Chiao Kuan-hua at UN*, United Nations; page 76 *stamp*, courtesy of Stanley Gibbons; *China's first hydrogen bomb*, China Pictorial, Dec. 1967; page 78 *opening Tan Zam railway*, Keystone Press Agency; page 79 *President Nyerere and Chou En-lai* Camera Press; page 84 *Lien Pi at Brussels,1975,* Commission of European Community, London Office.

Extracts

Source 3 J. O. P. Bland and E. Backhouse, *China under the Empress Dowager*, Heinemann, 1910, pp. 480-1
Source 4 Katherine A. Carl, *With the Empress Dowager of China*, Eveleigh Nash, 1906, p. 101
Source 5 Charles Meyer and Ian Allen, *Source Materials in Chinese History*, Frederick Warne, 1970, pp. 120-1
Source 7 R. C. North, *Chinese Communism*, Weidenfeld and Nicolson, 1969, pp. 101-4
Sources 9, 20 Jan Myrdal, *Report from a Chinese Village,* Heinemann, 1965, pp. 68-9 and p. 48.
Extracts in Chapter 2 from Agnes Smedley, *The Great Road,* Monthly Review Press, 1956, pp. 313-4;
and Dick Wilson, *The Long March,* Hamish Hamilton, 1971
Source 11 General and Madame Chiang Kai-shek, *A Fortnight in Sian*, Doubleday, Doran Inc., 1937, pp. 123-149
Sources 13,18 Edgar Snow, *Red Star Over China*, Victor Gollancz, 1969, pp. 285-9, 170-1
Source 15 John Gittings, *A Chinese View of China*, BBC Publications, 1973
Source 16 R. & N. Lapwood, *Through the Chinese Revolution*, Spalding and Levy, 1954, p. 29
Source 17 Jack Belden, *China Shakes the World*, Victor Gollancz, 1950, p. 169
Source 19 Myra Roper, *China in Revolution, 1911-1949*, Edward Arnold,1971
Sources 26,28 Bao Ruo-wang and Rudolph Chelminski, *Prisoner of Mao*, Andre Deutsch, 1975, p. 22
Source 27 In Winberg Chai (ed) *Essential Works of Chinese Communism*, Pica Press, 1970, pp. 332-3